The War on the Eastern Front

Defending Moscow in the summer of 1941.

The War on the Eastern Front

The Soviet Union 1941–1945
A Photographic History

Alexander Hill

Foreword by David Stahel

Pen & Sword
MILITARY

First published in Great Britain in 2021 by
PEN & SWORD MILITARY
an imprint of Pen & Sword Books Ltd
Yorkshire – Philadelphia

ISBN 978-1-52678-610-4

Typeset by Concept, Huddersfield, West Yorkshire, HD4 5JL.
Printed and bound in England by CPI Group (UK) Ltd, Croydon CR0 4YY.

Pen & Sword Books Ltd incorporates the Imprints of Aviation, Atlas, Family History,
Fiction, Maritime, Military, Discovery, Politics, History, Archaeology, Select, Wharncliffe
Local History, Wharncliffe True Crime, Military Classics, Wharncliffe Transport,
Leo Cooper, The Praetorian Press, Remember When, White Owl, Seaforth Publishing and
Frontline Books.

For a complete list of Pen & Sword titles please contact
PEN & SWORD BOOKS LTD
47 Church Street, Barnsley, South Yorkshire, S70 2AS, England
E-mail: enquiries@pen-and-sword.co.uk
Website: www.pen-and-sword.co.uk
or
PEN & SWORD BOOKS
1950 Lawrence Rd, Havertown, PA 19083, USA
E-mail: uspen-and-sword@casematepublishers.com
Website: www.penandswordbooks.com

Contents

Acknowledgements

Although the acknowledgements for this book are shorter than for some of my other works, I would like to take the opportunity to thank a few key individuals, without whom this project would not have come to fruition. First of all, I would certainly like to thank Ralph Gibson of RIA-Novosti (branded as Sputnik in the West) for making this project possible at all by making the selection of photographs presented here available to me at a viable cost. Having drawn on Sputnik's excellent photo archive for a number of other projects, I was keen to see more of the photos I had come across be published in the West as part of a publication such as this one. Ralph's enthusiasm for and commitment to the project when I proposed it to him has certainly been a valuable asset.

Having obtained the photographs for this book, I then sought out a publisher. Rupert Harding of Pen & Sword had asked me on a number of occasions over the years whether I'd like to write a book for them, and in this instance I was happy to oblige. Rupert successfully made the case for the book with his colleagues, and has been supportive of the whole endeavour from start to finish.

I would also like to thank Sarah Cook for her competent editing of my manuscript for the publisher, and the typesetter Noel Sadler for doing such a great job at showing off the photos in this book. Also to be thanked is Aaron Bates for his willingness to take a look at the proofs to look for any errors that might have made their way into the text. David Stahel kindly agreed to write a foreword for the book, and I very much appreciate the time and effort both Aaron and David have put in.

As is the convention with such books, I am pointing out that any errors or omissions are of course my responsibility. To close, I hope that you appreciate reading and browsing this book as much as I have selecting the photos and writing the captions!

Alexander Hill
Okotoks, Alberta
February 2021

Foreword

As an 18-year-old first-year history undergraduate I discovered the Nazi-Soviet War on the shelves of my university library. From the beginning I was gripped by the impossible scale, the frightful brutality and the mysterious absence of this unknown war in my decidedly Anglo-American education of the Second World War. I waded through the dense histories of Albert Seaton (*The Russo-German War*) and John Erickson (*The Road to Stalingrad*) without always understanding what I was reading. The military ranks, units and structures were assumed knowledge that I didn't possess. I'd never heard of most of the place-names and even major cities like Stalingrad were nowhere to be found in the family atlas. The cast of German and Soviet generals was too great to make sense of – I could never remember who was where or what they commanded. It was like some terribly overblown epic with a hopelessly convoluted plot and an unrelenting overindulgence in violence. Nevertheless, I felt compelled to read on because underlying all that I did not know was the one thing that I did – these horrific events were all real. Armies of millions of men battered away at each other for years in Eastern Europe to decide the outcome of the greatest war in history. Although I didn't know it then, my discovery of the Nazi-Soviet War was something of a rupture in my young life. My early fascination never really subsided and the old refrain that the more knowledge one has the more questions one asks was never more true.

As many devoted readers will know, studying the history of this war can be a solitary path. More than once I've been asked if the subject matter does not, at times, depress me. Perhaps it should. Perhaps the understandable aversion most people feel towards these events is part of what keeps us from repeating them. But I'm also sure that reading and writing about them provides its own essential warning from history. Books, army files, official papers, military documents, letters and diaries might record the fate of millions, but they are consumed in isolation and experienced individually. If nothing else, war is a highly emotional encounter, impossible to fully appreciate through history, but perhaps only in hindsight earning an essential objectivity. Giving voice to this past – or in the current context giving it a face – is a responsibility governed by a strict discipline of study that informs all of the very best histories and historians. Alexander Hill is one who has mastered this craft and here he brings to light a new and exciting collection of photographs that tell their own story of the Red Army's war, sometimes in ways words cannot. It is an invaluable record that charts some remarkable dimensions to this conflict and stands among the very best visual records of this great war. While we each experience the Nazi-Soviet War in unique ways, in an increasingly polarized world perhaps the simplicity of the static image reminds us of what the people who made up the Soviet Union sacrificed to defeat the scourge of Nazism.

David Stahel
The University of New South Wales, Canberra
April 2021

Introduction

The Great Patriotic War of 1941–1945 was both a traumatic and a formative experience for many tens of millions of the citizens of the Soviet Union. The figure of 27 million that is now commonly given for Soviet war-related deaths does not do justice to the collective suffering that the war brought on the Soviet peoples – a figure that includes many millions of Soviet Jews killed as part of the Final Solution or Holocaust. In the aftermath of the war, for a Soviet survivor not to have known of someone who had lost their life would have been the exception rather than the norm – a far cry from the situation for the Western Allies. The war might have ended in 1945, but as Belorussian Nobel Laureate Svetlana Alexievich recalled in *The Unwomanly Face of War*, her post-war childhood in many ways revolved around the memory of one war and preparations for the next one, with the absence of men thanks to the war a stark reality. She recalled:

> The village of my postwar childhood was a village of women. Village women. I don't remember any men's voices … They weep. Their songs are like weeping.
> In the school library half of the books were about the war. The same with the village library, and in the nearby town … Now I know the reason why … We were making war all the time, or preparing for war. Remembering how we made war.[1]

Although during the Cold War the Soviet contribution to the defeat of the Axis alliance was played down in the West, since the collapse of the Soviet Union in 1991 this has been less so. Western readers now have far greater access to a broader range of quality historical work on the Soviet experience of its part of the Second World War – still known today in Russia and many former Soviet republics as the Great Patriotic War. This broader range of work has been made possible to a large extent by the opening up of Soviet-era archives, and those archives have included not only historical documents but also photographs. This book takes advantage of this greater post-Soviet availability of Soviet photographs to provide what is arguably the most comprehensive photographic history of the Great Patriotic War available outside the former Soviet Union.

The photographs used in this book have been provided by the Russian news agency RIA-Novosti – now known in the West as Sputnik. The organisation on which RIA-Novosti is founded has been through many incarnations over the years, but can ultimately be traced back to the *Sovinformbiuro* of the period of the Great Patriotic War. The Soviet Information Bureau (*Sovetskoe informatsionnoe biuro* in Russian – typically shortened to *Sovinformbiuro*) was formed on 24 June 1941 two days after the German-led invasion of the Soviet Union had begun on the orders of the Communist Party of the Soviet Union and Soviet government. The *Sovinformbiuro* was to be an umbrella organisation to provide official information and sanctioned reporting on the war for both the Soviet people and foreign news outlets. Within the Soviet Union daily radio reports on the war by the *Sovinformbiuro* that began on 25 June 1941 ran until 15 May 1945 and were listened to by millions, with their announcer Iurii Levitan becoming a household name. Also becoming household names were many of the journalists who worked under the auspices of the *Sovinformbiuro*, including Konstantin Simonov, Mikhail Sholokhov and Il'ia Ehrenburg. Less famous, but no less significant in their work, were the many photographers also working ultimately for the *Sovinformbiuro* who took thousands of pictures and risked their lives to get their photographic record of the war. Photographers such as Max Alpert, Evgenii Khaldei and Mikhail Trakhman did not become household names in the same way as their literary counterparts, but with their cameras made what is arguably an as significant, if not more so, contribution to chronicling the war as their counterparts armed with their typewriters. Many of their photographs were published at home or abroad – being provided to foreign news outlets and governments as well as the Soviet press. Many of the pictures that were taken were, however, far too raw or honest in their portrayals of what was going on at the front or in the rear for them to be published during the war or during the Soviet period. Although some of those photographs have since then found their way into publications in the West, many have not, and certainly not as part of a single-volume collection such as this.

In its twenty-four chapters this book uses the photographs in the archives of the RIA-Novosti press agency inherited from the *Sovinformbiuro* to chart the course of the Soviet Union's wartime experiences. It does so starting with Soviet preparations for war in the 1930s and the small-war precursors to the Great Patriotic War of the late 1930s and 1940, before examining in some detail the titanic struggle that was the Great Patriotic War itself. It concludes with a final chapter looking at the aftermath of the war and its commemoration. Each chapter is provided with an introduction to set the scene for the photographs in that chapter, with each photograph being provided with a caption – some relatively brief but many providing more significant detail on what the photograph shows or on the context in which it is to be understood. In providing the reader with the introductions and captions, I have made use of much of my own work, with page references to those works provided in brackets in the text. In particular I have referred to *The Red Army and the Second World War* (Cambridge University Press, 2017), abbreviated as RASWW, and *The Great Patriotic War of the Soviet Union, 1941–45: A documentary reader* (Routledge, 2009), abbreviated as GPW. I have also made reference on occasion to other sources, and those references are provided in the short list of endnotes at the end of the book. For those looking to delve deeper into the content of particular chapters, in addition to being able to follow up on references in my own and other works that have been referenced, I have provided a Further Reading section by chapter at the end of the book with some suggestions for those wanting more detail on a particular topic or theme.

This collection of photographs is a testimony to the sacrifices made by the Soviet peoples in the defeat of Nazi Germany and her allies. As such, it seemed appropriate that its publication be linked to another recent memorialisation of the efforts of the Soviet peoples, namely the Soviet War Memorial in London. As part of the marking of the 50th Anniversary of Allied victory over Nazi Germany, the Russian Embassy in London asked the UK Society for Co-operation in Russian and Soviet Studies to organise services at the graves of Soviet service personnel in the UK. That request soon developed into a plan to erect a national memorial to Soviet citizens who lost their lives in the war against Nazi Germany and her allies, and which has ultimately resulted in the physical memorial that now stands in Geraldine Mary Harmsworth Park adjacent to the Imperial War Museum in Southwark, London. When I agreed to write this book for Pen & Sword, the publisher kindly agreed to make a donation to the Soviet War Memorial Trust. As part of that contract, the Soviet War Memorial Trust also has the opportunity to purchase copies of the book at a trade price and sell them as part of its ongoing fundraising efforts to maintain the memorial and organise events and educational activities relating to it. If you have purchased this book through them, you will have made a further contribution to the ongoing work of the trust by doing so.

Regardless of any political turmoil in governmental relations between the former Allies in the war against the Axis, it is important to remember and celebrate the wartime alliance between the Soviet Union and Western allies, and the sacrifices made by the Soviet peoples in securing victory. This book will hopefully contribute to maintaining that memory of events and the people who participated in them.

Alexander Hill
Okotoks, near Calgary, Canada
1 February 2021

'Wait for me'

By Konstantin Simonov

Simonov's 1941 wartime poem 'Wait for me' is undoubtedly one of the most famous pieces of artistic work to come out of the Great Patriotic War (see p. 186). The original Russian version, along with this author's own very liberal translation of the poem that aims to get across the original's sentiments as best as possible in English, are reproduced here. Alongside the photographs in this book, Simonov's poem is a memorial to the sacrifices made by the Soviet people during the Great Patriotic War.

Жди меня, и я вернусь.	Wait for me, and I'll be back.
Только очень жди,	Only be sure to wait,
Жди, когда наводят грусть	Wait, when the pollen-laden rains
Желтые дожди,	bring forth their gloom,
Жди, когда снега метут,	Wait, when the snow is swirling,
Жди, когда жара,	Wait, in the baking sun,
Жди, когда других не ждут,	Wait, when others can wait no more,
Позабыв вчера.	And when yesterday has been forgotten.
Жди, когда из дальних мест	Wait, when letters fail to arrive
Писем не придет,	from places far away,
Жди, когда уж надоест	Wait, when those waiting with you
Всем, кто вместе ждет.	Cannot wait another day.
Жди меня, и я вернусь,	Wait for me, and I'll be back,
Не желай добра	Do not harbour enmity,
Всем, кто знает наизусть,	For those who do not fail to tell you,
Что забыть пора.	That the time has come to forget.
Пусть поверят сын и мать	Let my mother, and my son,
В то, что нет меня,	convince themselves that I am gone,
Пусть друзья устанут ждать,	Let my friends tire of waiting,
Сядут у огня,	Sitting round the fire,
Выпьют горькое вино	Drinking bitter wine
На помин души ...	Reminding themselves of the past ...
Жди. И с ними заодно	Wait! Do not hasten to join with them
Выпить не спеши.	In drinking to one now gone.
Жди меня, и я вернусь,	Wait for me, and I'll be back.
Всем смертям назло.	Death will not have his wicked way.

Кто не ждал меня, тот пусть
Скажет: – Повезло.
Не понять, не ждавшим им,
Как среди огня
Ожиданием своим
Ты спасла меня.
Как я выжил, будем знать
Только мы с тобой, –
Просто ты умела ждать,
Как никто другой.

Let those who did not wait for me
Say simply that he cheated death.
They will not understand,
Not having waited, how
in the face of strife it was you,
You that saved me.
Only you and I will know,
How it was that I survived,
For solely you knew how to wait,
You, and you alone.

Chapter 1

The Red Army Prepares for War

The Great Patriotic War of the Soviet Union of 1941–1945 was fought by a Soviet Red Army that in many senses had been preparing for war for more than a decade when the German-led Axis invasion began on 22 June 1941. Although it was the October Revolution and Civil War in Russia of 1917–1921 that brought the Bolsheviks to power, in some ways the real revolution or a second revolution in Russia took place under Stalin. The collectivisation of agriculture and rapid industrialisation of the Soviet Union under Stalin undoubtedly led to a revolutionary transformation in the lives of many Soviet citizens, and particularly the peasantry, for whom many authors suggest that collectivisation of agriculture brought about a second serfdom. This second revolution not only advanced the goals of the October Revolution in leading to a growth in the proletariat or urban working class, but also in strengthening Soviet power. The collectivisation of agriculture in the Soviet Union that began in earnest in 1929 was geared to paying for industrialisation, and industrialisation was to a considerable extent about military power. In February 1931 Stalin gave what has become a famous and seemingly prescient speech to industrial managers, in which he pointed out:

> One feature of the history of Old Russia was the continual beating she suffered because of her backwardness. She was beaten by the Mongol Khans. She was beaten by the Turkish beys. She was beaten by the Swedish feudal lords. She was beaten by the Polish and Lithuanian gentry. She was beaten by the British and French capitalists. She was beaten by the Japanese barons. All beat her – because of her backwardness: because of her military backwardness, cultural backwardness, political backwardness, industrial backwardness, agricultural backwardness. They beat her because it was profitable and could be done with impunity ...
> That is why we must no longer lag behind ...
> We are fifty to a hundred years behind the advanced countries. We must make good this distance in ten years. Either we do it, or they crush us. [GPW, p. 9]

Although the Soviet Union still lacked concrete threats at this point beyond a vague notion that the capitalist powers would seek to undermine it, the expansion of Soviet military capabilities need not only have had a defensive purpose, but could also have allowed the Soviet Union to spread revolution by force of arms should conducive circumstances arise. Such an eventuality was something considered in the economic planning process – a powerful Red Army would be valuable regardless of the circumstances. Ultimately, according to Marxist-Leninist theory, the Russian Revolution would only be secure if there was revolution elsewhere, and the Soviet Union was committed to helping that along. Japanese expansion in the Far East, starting with Manchuria in 1931, soon gave the Soviet Union a concrete threat to focus on, although the Japanese threat alone was hardly existential. What was to become existential was the threat from fascism in Europe, and in particular the threat from a Nazi Germany that made it plain that eastward expansion was on its agenda, and that the Treaty of Versailles was not going to impede its territorial ambitions.

By 1936 the Red Army was arguably the most powerful army in Europe, although the purges launched against the Red Army and wider Soviet society in 1936–1938 did much to undermine gains that had been made. It is in many ways ironic that purges launched to supposedly make Stalin's regime more secure in the face of largely imagined foreign-backed internal opposition did so much to weaken the Red Army at the end of the 1930s. Perhaps fortunately for the Soviet Union, war with Nazi Germany was delayed by the signing of the Nazi-Soviet Pact and associated protocols of August–September 1939. Although during the spring of 1941 the Red Army was in the throes of expansion and reorganisation, it was back on a track towards greater military effectiveness. This improvement was thanks to some soul searching about the Red Army's performance in some of the small wars it was involved in during the late 1930s and 1940, and particularly the war with Finland of 1939–1940. These small wars preceding the Great Patriotic War will be considered in Chapters 2 and 3. This first chapter takes us more broadly through the 1930s and up to 1941 in visually highlighting key elements in the development of the Red Army and Soviet preparations for future war during the period prior to the beginning of the Great Patriotic War.

Sputnik 28932. It is perhaps appropriate that in this first photograph captured First World War-vintage 'Rikardo' Type B tanks (British Mark Vs) of the Red Army are shown on parade in Red Square on 7 November 1930 – the date of the 13th anniversary of the Russian Revolution according to the new post-revolutionary calendar. The First World War had been the final factor weakening the Tsarist regime in Russia to such an extent that it collapsed. That at the beginning of the new decade the Red Army was using such tanks in a parade highlights just how far behind the British and French the Soviet Union was at the start of the 1930s in terms of the development of armoured vehicles. At this time Weimar Germany was not allowed tanks under the Treaty of Versailles of 1919, although was secretly involved in developing tanks with the Soviet Union after Germany and the Soviet Union had come to terms under the 1922 Treaty of Rapallo. The Soviet Union's Tsarist predecessor had fought the First World War without any tanks at all – with the first tanks seeing action on Russian soil during the 1917–1921 Russian Civil War. Nonetheless, at the time this photograph was taken the first of the Soviet Union's Five-Year Plans was under way, and mass production of the first Soviet tanks was on the horizon. Stalin – now clearly the Soviet Union's leader – was determined that the Soviet Union would be able not only to defend itself, but perhaps even export its revolution abroad by force of arms. What the Soviet Union would also develop during the early 1930s was a military doctrine in which the new tanks would play a central role as the Red Army moved from relying on cavalry as the principle manoeuvre arm, to the tank.

Sputnik 21824. Here cavalry of the Central Asian Military District are shown on the move somewhere in Kazakhstan in 1932. Despite the development of tanks, the cavalry would continue to rival the armoured forces within the Red Army in terms of prestige until the mid-1930s. Cavalry had proven well-suited to the manoeuvrings of the Russian Civil War when the railway and the horse had proven so essential for all sides. Cavalry also proved valuable in the post-Civil War Red Army for many reasons, including the fact that many of the Red Army's territorial and regular forces were more familiar with the horse than the combustion engine, where most recruits were poorly educated peasants. Cavalry also proved valuable in the counter-insurgencies conducted by Soviet forces during the interwar period, including against the Basmachi resistance movement that was initially largely neutralised on Soviet soil in the early 1920s but that saw a resurgence in the late 1920s and early 1930s. Basmachi forces were able to briefly operate against the Soviet Union from Afghan territory at the end of the 1920s, during the suppression of which Soviet cavalry operated within northern Afghanistan.

Sputnik 87898. A key proponent of the cavalry arm within the Red Army was Semen Budennii, pictured here as Marshal of the Soviet Union in June 1938 as the so-called 'Great Purges' raged within Soviet society and the Red Army. Budennii's hostility towards Marshal Mikhail Tukha- chevskii – who was an early victim of the purges of the Red Army in June 1937 – was not something that Budennii concealed, and seems to have at least in part been as a result of Tukhachevskii's support for the mechanisation of the Red Army as part of the development of the concepts of 'Deep Battle' and 'Deep Operations'. 'Deep Battle' – and its larger-scale compatriot 'Deep Operations' – shared much with the later much-vaunted German Blitzkrieg, whereby tanks, supported by artil- lery, aircraft and even airborne forces, would punch through enemy defences and break into the rear, where they would paralyse the enemy response to the offensive operations. Despite the deaths of Tukhachevskii and many of his colleagues, Budennii was unable to halt the mechanisation of the Red Army even if his position within the chain of command no doubt played a part in the continued importance of the cavalry arm in the Red Army into the Great Patriotic War.

Sputnik 3324617. The Soviet armed forces in 1930 were not only dependent on equipment manufactured before the revolution in terms of tanks and other equipment for the army, but also for naval forces. Here 'Novik' Class destroyers are shown with what appears to be a Polikarpov R-1 aircraft on manoeuvres during the summer of 1930. These vessels had been built or laid down by the Tsarist regime, with the Bolsheviks completing a number of such vessels after the revolution. In 1930 Bolshevik naval power was limited to the Baltic and Black Seas, but the 1930s would see the emergence of flotillas that would become fleets in both the north and Far East. Although ambitious Soviet plans for naval development during the 1930s would not come to fruition because increasing attention had to be paid to the readying of ground and air forces for war on the Eurasian landmass, the Soviet Navy would by the start of the Great Patriotic War be equipped with a mixture of ships of both Tsarist and Soviet construction. The Polikarpov aircraft in the photo was one of the first mass-produced aircraft in the Soviet Union, although it was derived from flyable British Airco/ de Havilland D.H.4 aircraft captured during the Russian Civil War. The 1930s would see the mass production of genuinely Soviet aircraft.

Sputnik 60300. By 1936 the Red Army had been, particularly materially, transformed. Tanks such as the T-26s shown here on exercises in the spring of that year in the Krasnoiarsk region in Siberia were available in their thousands. More than a thousand early T-26s had been produced by the end of the First Five-Year Plan in 1932, with 1936 alone seeing the manufacture or completion of just over 1,300 more [RASWW, p. 37]. Whether the tanks and their crews – as part of formations of increasing size – were capable of putting 'Deep Operations' or even 'Deep Battle' into effect was, however, another matter. Notice the rail-like aerial around the turret on the lead and second tanks in this picture. Most of the remaining tanks lack radio communications, meaning that communication between the command tanks and the remainder of the unit would mean reliance on visual signals. If a command tank was to be knocked out, in all probability a unit would be unable to communicate with its headquarters. Communications would be one of a number of impediments to the implementation of 'Deep Battle'. Soon, however, as Tukhachevskii and those of his colleagues who were the architects of 'Deep Battle' were purged, the Red Army would move temporarily towards a focus on the tank as primarily being a means of supporting the infantry. Manoeuvres such as those shown here were often not particularly realistic in recreating anything like actual wartime conditions. Tightly choreographed, such manoeuvres during the 1930s were more about impressing foreign observers and the top brass rather than preparing troops for the chaos of battle.

(*Opposite*) Sputnik 3029276. Another shot of a T-26 from 1936, this time taken during manoeuvres in the summer of that year in the Moscow region. Other than showing off some of the relatively ornate woodwork on this peasant's cottage and indeed providing a close-up of the front portion of the tank, the picture in many ways encapsulates key contrasts in the Soviet Union at the time. One contrast evident in this picture is between industrialisation and the development of a modern Red Army and the continued existence of a peasant majority that in many ways was living under a new serfdom in the form of collectivisation. Also, as many young people were receiving an education denied to their forebears and often looked towards a new life in the growing cities and urban settlements, something of a chasm existed in Soviet society not just between the urban and rural, but between younger and older generations. Note that this tank has a radio aerial indicating a command vehicle. Note also the machine gun mounted alongside the very respectable-for-the-time main armament in the form of a relatively high-velocity 45mm gun capable of penetrating more than 35mm of vertical armour at a range of 1km with an armour-piercing round.

(*Above*) Sputnik 103315. An impressive array of Soviet TB-3 bombers in early 1934. In the 'Deep Battle' and 'Deep Operations' schema the heavy bomber was to play its part in the breakthrough and exploitation by ground forces by hitting enemy communications and infrastructure deeper in the enemy rear, and thus contributing to the degradation of the enemy's ability to deal with a Soviet penetration of their lines. Alongside tanks the TB-3 heavy bomber was often used to symbolise the transformation and modernisation of the Soviet armed forces during the mid-1930s. Used as both a bomber and transport aircraft for paratroops, the TB-3 was when introduced an advanced design that would establish a configuration for heavy bombers that would be the norm throughout the period of the piston-engined aircraft. Although still in service at the beginning of the Great Patriotic War – and consequently compared to Allied heavy bombers available during the early part of the Second World War – its contemporaries in terms of design were the somewhat antiquated Curtiss B-2 and Handley-Page Heyford bombers that were vastly inferior. As with other aircraft types, any Soviet advantages in terms of capabilities gained through being pioneers in new design features had been lost by the end of the decade. However, whereas the Soviet Union would introduce new fighter aircraft during the Great Patriotic War that would match or exceed the capabilities of those of their opponents, the Soviet heavy bomber force would not advance beyond the already inadequate at the time of series production pre-war successor to the TB-3, the Pe-8.

(*Above*) Sputnik 3045682. Often shown jumping from modified TB-3 bombers, this photo of September 1935 shows Soviet paratroopers descending towards and having landed on open terrain in the Kiev region of the Ukraine. Like the bomber aircraft from which they would typically jump, at this time the Soviet Union was ahead of its would-be competitors in terms of the development of airborne forces. In the 'Deep Battle' schema such troops dropped en masse in the enemy rear would in theory be used to further paralyse any enemy response to the breakthrough of ground forces. Subsequently, only rarely during the Great Patriotic War were Soviet paratroops employed in their intended role, where their opponents and allies had taken an idea that the Soviet Union had pioneered and developed it. Soviet enthusiasm for airborne forces would, however, return with something of a vengeance during the Cold War.

(*Opposite, above*) Sputnik 5781688. One area in which the Soviet Union had considerable pre-revolutionary stocks of weaponry that would still be useful in future wars was in light and medium artillery. In addition, the Soviet Union would manufacture Tsarist-era guns in order to get production under way before new designs could be produced. This photo shows a 122mm Model 1910/1930 gun with horses and limber on parade in Red Square in Moscow on the 18th anniversary of the Revolution in 1935. Soviet production of this gun differed from the earlier Tsarist version in terms of the sights, and in the modified carriage on the Soviet production model that was in fact simplified. Only some of the guns would end up with metal wheels with rubber tires, without which they could only be towed at a maximum speed of 6km/h! Although the Red Army strove towards greater mechanisation, the infantry divisions in particular continued to rely on the horse into and throughout the Great Patriotic War. This gun equipped the artillery regiments of many infantry divisions at the beginning of the Great Patriotic War.

(*Overleaf*) Sputnik 24690. Although the Red Army put considerable existing stocks of artillery to good use – and produced their own versions of Tsarist-era guns – the addition of modern artillery for the Red Army was a key goal for the military elements of the five-year plans for Soviet industry of the 1930s. Indeed, in 1929 the Communist Party had dictated that the Red Army should have technology more advanced than that of potential opponents by the end of the First Five-Year Plan in three key areas – for aircraft, tanks and artillery. [RASWW, p. 39] Although it would take a little longer to reach this point than proposed, as the T-26 tank and TB-3 bomber suggest, by the mid-1930s the Soviet Union was providing the Soviet armed forces with modern military equipment that exceeded foreign equivalents in terms of capability. To a lesser extent such a claim could be made regarding some of the newer artillery pieces being provided to the Red Army. Here, B-4 guns are shown on parade in Red Square in Moscow, this time on 1 May 1936, with the photograph being taken from the Kremlin side of the square. Such heavy artillery – very much suited for siege work and clearly developed in the light of First World War experience – absorbed considerable industrial resources at a time when there were very many competing demands for them. Although of little use early in the Great Patriotic War, as photographs later in this book will show, they had value in Finland in 1939–1940 in breaking through the Mannerheim Line defences, and again in urban warfare as the Red Army fought its way through fortified German towns and cities later in the Great Patriotic War.

(*Opposite, below*) Sputnik 5783245. This parade shot – taken in Red Square on 7 November 1938 on the 21st anniversary of the revolution – shows T-37 light amphibious tanks. Although the Soviet Union had in excess of 11,000 tanks in service by February 1938, many of these tanks were lighter models that had little value by that time when facing contemporary anti-tank weapons. At this point the Red Army had nearly 4,000 of these T-37 and similar T-38 tanks in service. [RASWW, p. 119 and p. 601 n. 36] Although in theory useful for reconnaissance – for which their amphibious capability was a particular asset – the absence of radios would in many cases mean that getting reconnaissance information back to those who could use it in a timely manner would be a significant problem. At the end of the 1930s the Soviet Union was looking to switch productive capacity to more heavily armoured and armed tanks.

(*Above*) Sputnik 2389825. During the 1930s not only were the five-year plans increasingly focused on the defence sector, but Soviet society was increasingly focused on the prospect of future war. In addition to those subject to compulsory military service receiving military training with the Red Army, Soviet citizens could receive some sort of military preparation – even if rudimentary – through the civil defence organisation typically known by the abbreviation form of its title, OSOAVIAKHIM. This picture shows civil defence training in progress in the spring of 1939 in the Ukraine. The threat of the use of chemical weapons seems to have been something of a recurring theme in such preparations, with the gas mask a far from unusual accoutrement to such activities. Although the value of such training was in many instances probably limited, OSOAVIAKHIM did offer programmes – sometimes in collaboration with the Komsomol or youth wing of the Communist Party – that were apparently popular with young people and that gave a select few the opportunity to learn to fly or receive parachute training.

(*Above*) Sputnik 662684. A key component in developing a modern, mechanised Red Army was education – be that prior to entering the Red Army or during service within it. Although this photograph shows students of the Military Academy for Motorisation and Mechanisation on 28 June 1941, the academy was created back in 1932. By the end of the 1930s not only were new recruits into the Red Army receiving longer educations than their predecessors the previous decade before donning their uniforms, but were far more likely to receive specialised military education beyond basic training once in the Red Army. Military commanders were much more likely to receive additional education as they progressed in rank than in the past, with the Academy of the General Staff created in 1936 being at the apex of the Red Army educational system. [RASWW, pp. 20, 49]

(*Opposite*) Sputnik 7381. Ironically, given the drive to increase educational levels within the Red Army during the 1930s, by the beginning of 1940 the purges of the Red Army in 1937–1938 had left a clique of senior military leaders in positions of authority who were poorly educated in military matters. This state of affairs was epitomised by People's Commissar for Defence and head of the armed forces, Kliment Voroshilov, who had no formal military education at all! After the débâcle in Finland covered in Chapter 3, Voroshilov was removed from his position as head of the armed forces, and there were signs that his clique was losing authority to younger commanders with more military education, such as the two Soviet military leaders shown here during exercises in the Kiev Military District in September 1940: Marshal Semen Timoshenko (*left*) and General Georgii Zhukov (*right*). Timoshenko and Zhukov amongst others would oversee something of a transformation in Red Army training and manoeuvres immediately prior to the Great Patriotic War away from the superficial and choreographed towards a better approximation of combat conditions. Zhukov would go on to become a Marshal of the Soviet Union and the only person in the Soviet Union other than Leonid Brezhnev to receive the prestigious Hero of the Soviet Union award four times.

Sputnik 634863. This photograph shows the new, more realistic training of the Red Army imme-diately prior to the Great Patriotic War. Here soldiers of the 70th Rifle Division advance through a smokescreen in the Leningrad region on 10 May 1941. Note the junior commander leading his troops – in distinct uniform and with only a pistol – making him a desirable target for any enemy soldier but particularly a sniper. During the Great Patriotic War the tendency would be for junior officers to look more like the soldiers they were fighting with to mitigate the risk of them being singled out for particular enemy attention. At the time this photograph was taken, although Stalin was attempting not to provoke Nazi Germany into attacking the Soviet Union by clearly mobilising for war, this was nonetheless brought about by a certain realisation of the possibility of German attack in the near future. A significant part of the Red Army was mobilised during this period, even if the Soviet Union had not ordered a general mobilisation. Although Stalin would subsequently suppress the notion that a German attack was imminent, nonetheless the Red Army continued to move units and formations to the West in late May and early June 1941 as it prepared for war – just not by Hitler's timetable. Having seen action in the war against Finland in 1939–1940, the 70th Rifle Division would begin the Great Patriotic War as a reserve division for forces facing the Finns, before being thrown into the maelstrom below Leningrad in early July as the Red Army sought to halt the German advance towards the city.[2]

Chapter 2

Preludes to the Main Event: the Soviet Union's Small Wars of the 1930s

As the Red Army grew during the second half of the 1930s and readied itself for future war, it would have a number of opportunities to fight against a range of opponents, from German and Italian-backed Nationalist forces in Spain to Japanese forces in China. Although few Soviet troops would participate in the Spanish Civil War, Soviet military equipment that included tanks and aircraft – often with 'volunteer' Soviet crews – would get its first meaningful combat testing from 1936. The following year Soviet 'volunteer' aircrews would for the first time face the Japanese in the Far East as Japan foolhardily expanded its commitments on the continent from Manchuria to the whole of China. As if the fighting with Chinese forces wasn't enough, local Japanese commanders took it upon themselves to pick fights with the Soviet Union both in 1938 on the Manchurian border with Soviet Far Eastern territory, and in 1939 on the Manchurian border with Soviet-backed Mongolia. In all of these instances Soviet lives were lost, but experience was accrued – with some of it even leading to meaningful and positive changes to wider Soviet preparations for future war in Europe. A good example here is in the development of tanks, where experience in the late 1930s highlighted how speed provided little defence alone for tanks with only weak armour against contemporary anti-tank guns, leading ultimately to the development and introduction of the KV-series and T-34 tanks for the

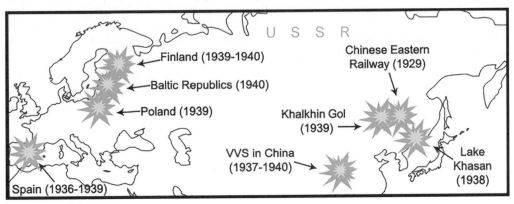

Soviet military engagements outside the Soviet Union, 1929–1940.

beginning of the next decade. All of this was unfortunately taking place under the cloud of the Great Purges of the Red Army in 1937–1938 that would hamper not only Red Army operations but also the processing of combat experience that was being accrued. This chapter looks at the nature of Soviet participation in some of those conflicts, and in particular in the fighting against Japan on the Soviet and Mongolian borders in 1938–1939.

Sputnik 6226. Soviet cameraman and later director Roman Karmen with Republican troops in September 1936 during the early phases of the Spanish Civil War. Karmen made his way to Spain slightly ironically via Berlin and then Paris – the latter stop required him to obtain a Spanish visa since at that time the Soviet Union didn't even have diplomatic relations with Spain. Of note apparently en route was Karmen's first encounter with bananas – which he had never tried before – and in Berlin the sight of 'live fascists'![3] The Spanish Civil War was undoubtedly a major milestone for Soviet fears of actual rather than imagined war on the European continent. With their interventions in the Spanish Civil War it became apparent that Nazi Germany and fascist Italy were going to be able to support the Nationalist rebels in Spain without meaningful sanction by Britain and France. If Britain and France were not going to act against fascism in Europe then a showdown between fascism and Soviet communism was becoming all the more likely. The Soviet Union did provide some support to the Republican government in Spain, with Soviet military personnel serving alongside Republican forces as pilots, tank crew and advisers for example, although as 'volunteers' nominally not serving as Red Army personnel. However, Stalin was keen not to provoke either all-out war with the fascist powers, or perhaps more importantly at this point a falling-out with Britain and France, who it was hoped would be willing to join the Soviet Union in curtailing fascist ambitions in Europe. There was certainly a relationship between the Spanish Civil War and the Great Purges in the Soviet Union, where the former seems to have provoked Stalin to believe that it was necessary to put his domestic house in order if there was an increasing threat of a war that his enemies might use as an opportunity to undermine or overthrow him.

Sputnik 104299. This Soviet poster of 1938 by artist Boris Prorokov is nominally concerned with the 24th International Day of Youth associated with the Young Communist International and International Union of Socialist Youth. The caption reads 'For peace, freedom and democracy, against fascism and war!' Those fighting fascism in the poster are a young Spanish republican and Chinese soldier. In 1937 Japanese forces, having invaded Manchuria in 1931, invaded the remainder of China. Once again, as in Spain, relatively small numbers of Soviet 'volunteers' would fight alongside the Chinese, with Soviet aircraft and aircrews being the most significant contribution.

Sputnik 59244. In this picture Soviet commanders are shown surveying the scene at Lake Khasan on the Soviet-Manchurian border at the end of July 1938, at the beginning of the Lake Khasan incident. The Lake Khasan border incident saw significant localised fighting between Soviet and Japanese forces that ended in the Soviet Union being able to assert its border claims after a two-week period of conflict. Although typically described as a border incident because the fighting over boundaries was geographically so constrained, this incident was far from being a skirmish, with a significant part of a Soviet corps (39th Rifle Corps) being committed against a sizeable portion of a Japanese division (19th Division).

(*Above*) Sputnik 44392. A slightly later photograph showing Red Army soldiers near Lake Khasan in early August 1938, at which point Japanese troops were occupying higher ground that they had seized from Soviet border troops at the end of July. That Soviet forces were successful in asserting Soviet claims on territory in the region owed more to a lack of Japanese commitment to the fighting than to Soviet competence. During the summer of 1938 the purges of the Red Army were still in full swing and had hit Soviet forces in the region hard, and undoubtedly had an impact on Soviet military effectiveness. Nonetheless, local Japanese commanders did not receive the same level of support from their superiors as their Soviet counterparts, where Japanese leaders higher up the chain of command were keen to prevent an escalation in the fighting. Japanese forces were not only outnumbered during the Lake Khasan fighting, but also operating without air support, and would eventually withdraw from the battlefield after having been pushed back at heavy cost for the Red Army rather than being resoundingly defeated. During the fighting near Lake Khasan at least 717 Soviet troops were killed, with a further 75 missing, along with 2,752 wounded. On the Japanese side in the region of 526 were killed and 913 wounded. [RASWW, p. 88]

(*Opposite*) Sputnik 40949. A Soviet Red Banner is flown over Zaozernaia Hill towards the end of the Lake Khasan fighting, where a ceasefire was implemented the following day on 11 August. The terrain over which the fighting took place is shown well in this photo, with a combination of low-lying wet terrain and craggy outcrops higher up being far from suitable for the deployment of tanks. Nonetheless, the Red Army would deploy the tanks of the 2nd Mechanized Brigade along with those organic to the 32nd Rifle Division during the fighting. Given the terrain it is unsurprising that, despite the limited number of anti-tank weapons on the Japanese side, as Soviet tanks advanced on 6–7 August after Japanese positions had been softened up by Soviet bombers only 'individual tanks made it to their objectives, but very few made it back. They got stuck in the marshes ...'. In order to prevent their capture by the Japanese 'four to five tanks were bombarded by their own artillery'. According to one Soviet source the Red Army lost twenty-four tanks outright with a further fifty-six damaged during fighting that in many ways did not show the Red Army in a favourable light. [RASWW, pp. 88–9]

(*Opposite, above*) Sputnik 61242. The following year another border incident – nominally between the Japanese and Mongolians – escalated into significant if localised fighting between Soviet, Mongolian and Japanese forces at Khalkhin Gol. This time, however, the terrain was far better suited to Soviet mechanised forces. Here, Soviet tankers are shown prior to combat operations with their BT-series tanks during an early period in the fighting. Although relatively lightly armoured, the BT-7s shown here were both capable of high speeds on suitable terrain and armed with a potent 45mm gun developed from the 45mm 20-K gun of the early 1930s. In the 'Deep Battle' schema of the mid-1930s such tanks were to be tasked with exploiting a breakthrough in enemy lines, but by the late 1930s it was becoming clear to Soviet military leaders that in practice designating tanks for specific battlefield roles did not always fit in with front-line needs and the availability of vehicles. At Khalkhin Gol such tanks would not only operate semi-independently as intended when they were conceived, but also in combination with and at the pace of the infantry (a photograph of which is available in RASWW, p. 99). Of note in this picture are the covers on some of the M1936 helmets being worn – something that was certainly not standard issue but fits in with a growing Soviet awareness of the need for camouflage and *maskirovka* ('concealment').

(*Opposite, below*) Sputnik 601334. The first of two shots of Soviet BT-series tanks at Khalkhin Gol, this time on the move. In this photo there is a mixture of earlier BT-5 and more recent BT-7 tanks, the former with the armour on the turret less well sloped. Although such tanks performed well enough at Khalkhin Gol against an opponent poorly prepared for anti-tank warfare, by the time German forces led the Axis invasion of the Soviet Union in June 1941 they were looking increasingly outdated compared to the modern anti-tank weapons typically available to German forces. At the beginning of April 1941 the Red Army would still have nearly 2,500 of the basic version of the BT-7 in service, along with approaching 2,000 equipped with radios – to which can be added nearly 1,500 earlier BT-5 and more than 500 BT-2 tanks.[4] Most of these tanks would be lost during the summer and autumn of 1941.

(*Above*) Sputnik 38695. Another shot of BT-series tanks 'in action' during the initial stages of the fighting at Khalkhin Gol. This photograph – apparently showing tanks hull-down behind the ridge of some shallow hills – gives a good sense of the terrain at Khalkhin Gol that would serve the Red Army so well and allow their tanks to successfully operate on the flanks of the Japanese forces. Although the Japanese would employ their own tanks early on, during the later stages of the fighting they would operate without armoured units. With relatively few anti-tank guns, in such terrain the Japanese had relatively few ways in which to effectively counter such Soviet tanks that had proven far more vulnerable in the face of light anti-tank guns in fighting over less tank-friendly terrain in Spain.

(*Opposite*) Sputnik 42389. The official caption for this photograph notes that it shows the commissar for an artillery *divizion* (not to be confused with division) giving the troops a political pep talk very early on in the Khalkhin Gol fighting on 5 June 1939. Their artillery piece is, once again as in Chapter 1, a 122mm Model 1910/1930 gun. Not only did the Red Army have a clear superiority in armour at Khalkhin Gol – and particularly during the later phases of the fighting – but enjoyed a superiority in artillery for most of the fighting as well. During what was in many ways a nineteenth-century set-piece battle fought with twentieth-century weapons, Soviet artillery was often firing directly on visible Japanese positions and from prepared Soviet positions – making fire control far easier than it would often be against German forces in more fluid circumstances in the near future.

(*Above*) Sputnik 39615. The Soviet infantry at Khalkhin Gol also had advantages over their Japanese counterparts, one of which was having a far more effective heavy machine gun than the Japanese Type 3 or 92. The ubiquitous Maxim Model 1910/1930 had served some of these Red Army men's fathers and grandfathers during the First World War, and like the similar British Vickers gun would serve them well during the Second World War. Although rather cumbersome, in a sustained fire role from defensive positions such machine guns continued to be as deadly to infantry as they had been in the First World War as long as they were kept supplied with ammunition. Note that the infantrymen behind the machine gunners are equipped only with rifles – submachine guns had yet to be adopted by the Red Army. Despite the increasingly modern weaponry being deployed in battle, the infantryman had still to be prepared to fight with his bayonet as affixed to the rifle in the right foreground of this picture.

(*Above*) Sputnik 41139. In overall command of Soviet forces at Khalkhin Gol prior to the arrival of Georgii Zhukov was Komandarm 2nd Rank Gregorii Shtern. Shtern was something of a rising star in the Red Army in the late 1930s, and the evidence suggests that he was at least a competent military leader. He had been the Head Soviet Adviser to Republican forces in Spain during 1937 and into early 1938, before commanding Soviet forces at Lake Khasan later that same year. Further promotion and a role as co-ordinator of Soviet forces in the Far East during the Khalkhin Gol

fighting followed, and he was awarded the prestigious title of Hero of the Soviet Union after the successful conclusion of the fighting there. Whilst his reputation was a little tarnished during the fighting in Finland in early 1940, this does not seem to have damaged his career, and he would command Soviet forces in the Far East from June 1940 through to the beginning of June 1941. Although Shtern had survived the period of intense purging of the Red Army command of 1937–1938, the purges continued at a reduced tempo into the first months of the Great Patriotic War. Despite having been awarded the title Hero of the Soviet Union less than two years earlier, Shtern was arrested on 7 June 1941 and executed in late October of that year, having been accused of the usual crime of participation in a Trotskyist conspiracy against Stalin and of spying for the Germans. That these charges lacked substance is evidenced by the fact that he was posthumously rehabilitated in 1954 after Stalin's death. The purging of the Soviet military leadership prior to the Great Patriotic War would undoubtedly hamper Soviet efforts to prepare for what was seen as the inevitable showdown with Nazi Germany. Note the attempts at camouflage of the position in this picture, where at Khalkhin Gol Red Army forces showed elements of a penchant for *maskirovka* that would be evident during the Great Patriotic War.

(*Above*) Sputnik 43033. A radio operator from an artillery unit joins the Young Communist organisation, the Komsomol, during the period of the Khalkhin Gol fighting. In the background are a pair of BA-20 armoured cars. Such armoured cars would play a meaningful role in the fighting in ensuring communications between Soviet units. Despite the contained nature of the Khalkhin Gol fighting, and opportunities for the use of field telephone communications, such communications were always subject to damage in the fighting, and the Red Army was poorly provided for with radios. In such circumstances communication between units and higher level command was frequently dependent on runners and commanders physically moving around the battlefield – often making use of armoured cars to provide at least some safety. Such armoured cars – with limited ground clearance – still had reasonable mobility on the grassland at Khalkhin Gol, although would largely be replaced by more mobile vehicles during the Great Patriotic War. A fairly staggering 133 Soviet armoured cars were lost at Khalkhin Gol, including 19 BA-20. [RASWW, p. 103]

(*Above*) Sputnik 40071. In command of Soviet forces during the later phases of operations on the ground at Khalkhin Gol – that is commanding the 57th Special Army Corps – was future Marshal of the Soviet Union Georgii Zhukov, seen here with other commanders in the Khalkhin Gol area. Although Soviet success here contributed to Zhukov's meteoric rise in the Red Army in the late 1930s and early 1940s, in his post-career memoirs he does not make much of his leadership at Khalkhin Gol. Whilst events there were certainly overshadowed by the Great Patriotic War, it is reasonable to surmise that Zhukov knew that success at Khalkhin Gol did not equate to battlefield success against the German Wehrmacht. At Khalkhin Gol the Japanese were outnumbered in terms of key indices such as artillery, and in general did not receive the relatively lavish material support that Red Army forces enjoyed, and were also ill-equipped for the sort of mechanised warfare that the Red Army and the Wehrmacht were preparing to fight in the late 1930s. The fighting at Khalkhin Gol was also constrained to a limited area, over which it was relatively easy to exercise command even with poor communications. Thus it is perhaps apparent why Zhukov seemed reticent to blow his own trumpet over a success that would soon be overshadowed by defeats at the hands of the Wehrmacht during the summer of 1941.

(*Opposite, above*) Sputnik 41135. Soviet pilots play dominoes during the early phases of the fighting at Khalkhin Gol. In the background their I-16 fighter aircraft stand waiting. When introduced in 1934, and particularly when up-engined, the I-16 was an advanced and capable aircraft. Flown by some of the better Soviet pilots available and operating over a confined area that did not tax Soviet command-and-control capabilities, Soviet air support at Khalkhin Gol proved relatively effective. Later model I-16s could certainly more than hold their own against the Ki-27 aircraft fielded by the Japanese, and continued to be a useful aircraft into the Second World War.

(*Opposite, below*) Sputnik 56153. One of the most significant Soviet achievements at Khalkhin Gol was logistical – sustaining a large force at a considerable distance from the Soviet European heartland. By the time Soviet forces launched their 20 August offensive that would lead to Japanese defeat, the 1st Army Group at Khalkhin Gol would consist of in the region of 57,000 troops. Communications both with and within Mongolia were poor, with the nearest railhead to Khalkhin Gol being some 700km away. One thing that the Soviet Union could do very well, however, was

focus effort and resources on a particular problem – and particularly where that was the only pressing problem at a given time. More than 6,000 motor vehicles allotted to the 57th Special Corps alone would help keep the corps fighting, at a time when the Red Army as a whole had a total of only 272,000 motor vehicles of all types. Aircraft had their role to play in the Soviet effort at Khalkhin Gol, where aircraft such as this licence-built DC-3 – in Soviet service the Li-2 – were used to fly in key personnel and supplies and fly out wounded, as shown here. In addition to losing nearly 10,000 killed, missing or who died from wounds in situ, a further 15,000 or more Soviet troops were wounded. From a similar strength force in terms of manpower, the Japanese would lose at least 8,000 killed and a slightly higher number wounded. [RASWW, pp. 102–5]

Chapter 3

Débâcles in Poland and Finland

More significant for the development of the Red Army than the Spanish Civil War or fighting against the Japanese in the Far East in 1937–1939 was the war against Finland, fought by the Soviet Union in late 1939 and early 1940. In August and September 1939 the Soviet Union signed the Molotov-Ribbentrop or Nazi-Soviet Pact and associated protocols that saw the Soviet Union and the Third Reich agree to carve up Poland and divide Eastern Europe into spheres of influence. For the Soviet Union the signing of the Pact was clearly a means to an end – to buy time before what was seen as an inevitable showdown with Nazi Germany. Just what the Soviet Union was buying time for has, however, been the subject of some debate. Soviet and post-Soviet Russian scholars have tended to portray the signing of the Pact as a measure simply designed to deflect German attentions from a peacefully inclined Soviet Union only interested in its own defence. That this defence seems to have required territorial acquisition – be that the eastern regions of Poland forcibly acquired in September 1939, or the Baltic Republics in June 1940 – was typically brushed over both at the time and in subsequent Soviet histories. Soviet defence also apparently required the acquisition of territory close to Leningrad from Finland, where Bolshevik leaders could remember how Finnish territory had been a springboard for German forces back in February 1918. It was the acquisition of this territory in particular during a costly war lasting from the end of November 1939 through to mid-March 1940 that provoked considerable soul-searching in the Soviet Union as to how the Red Army could be a better fighting force. During the war in Finland the Red Army lost in excess of 70,000 killed or died during casualty evacuation, with a further at least 16,292 who died in hospital and 39,369 missing in action and largely assumed killed. As such, the Red Army lost more than 125,000 troops in a very localised war against a much smaller and in many senses less well-equipped force, although the nearly 25,000 Finnish soldiers killed, missing and died from wounds speaks to the intensity of the fighting. [RASWW, p. 167] What Western accounts of the war tended to ignore was that the Red Army that performed so dismally in Finland in late 1939 had already shown improvement by the end of the war in mid-March 1940, and would continue to improve as the German invasion of 22 June 1941 approached. The more realistic training portrayed in Chapter 1 was just one of the results of the war with Finland.

Although Stalin and the Soviet leadership fully expected to go to war with Germany at some point in the future, after the signing of the Nazi-Soviet Pact it was hoped this would not be for some time. It was certainly hoped that Germany would get bogged down in war against Britain and France for a protracted period of time, allowing the Red Army to be readied for the inevitable showdown. Whether this showdown was supposed to involve the Soviet Union attacking Germany first is unclear, but there is certainly evidence that this was seen as a distinct possibility. In reality, Germany defeated British and French forces on the continent far more quickly than had been hoped for in Moscow. As Germany readied itself for war against the Soviet Union – despite not having knocked the British out of the war – Stalin seems to have tried to convince himself that Hitler would not be foolish enough to attack the Soviet Union. Certainly, with an 'active' Western Front and whilst the Soviet Union was providing Germany with the sort of raw materials it could hope to acquire if it invaded the Soviet Union, a German invasion did not seem to be a wise course of action to a Stalin who was assuming that Hitler was operating according to the logic of Realpolitik. Stalin, it seems, underestimated the role that ideology played in German foreign policy – an underestimation that would cost the Red Army dearly.

Sputnik 101829. In this photograph Soviet forces are shown passing through the village of Molochanka in what in Soviet terms was western Belorussia, in Polish terms eastern Poland, sometime after 17 September 1939. The Soviet invasion of Poland, which began on 17 September 1939, was hurriedly organised to take advantage of an opportunity offered by the Nazi-Soviet Pact signed only weeks before. The resulting Soviet advance was poorly organised. The photograph here shows an interesting mix of mechanised and horse-drawn elements of the Red Army. Throughout the Great Patriotic War Soviet infantry divisions would rely primarily on the horse. The armoured cars are BA-10 models, essentially a lightly armoured tank on wheels armed with a for the time potent 45mm gun. Although such armoured cars continued to be used throughout the Great Patriotic War, they were increasingly replaced in a reconnaissance role by either foreign-supplied light armoured vehicles or light tanks. The Red Army would meet only sporadic resistance as it occupied the eastern part of Poland, and particularly so in the border regions where the population was more likely to be ethnically Belorussian or Ukrainian.

Sputnik 25895. The official caption for this photo reads 'German military personnel chat with the commander of a Soviet tank regiment somewhere near Brest' – the date given being 20 September 1939. This clearly staged photo does not do justice to what must in many senses have been an uncomfortable meeting. Prior to the Nazi-Soviet Pact Nazi Germany had been vilified in the Soviet press, and all of a sudden it was effectively allied to the Soviet Union. What would now be termed 'friendly fire' incidents between German and Soviet forces can also not have helped the atmosphere as Soviet and German forces met. [e.g. RASWW, pp. 128–9] Whilst military personnel could easily find common ground through their professions, the ideological contexts in which the two armed forces were operating were very different.

(*Above*) Sputnik 432036. Another meeting apparently taking place on 20 September 1939, this time between Soviet and Polish soldiers. Whether this gathering continued to be quite as cordial as it appears after the photograph was taken is unclear. With much of the Polish armed forces fighting German forces, there were few Polish troops to oppose the Soviet advance. There were, however, a number of relatively small engagements between Soviet and Polish forces that led to losses on both sides. Because resistance was typically light – and perhaps because Soviet troops believed the propaganda that they would be met with open arms by those they were 'liberating' during their rapid advance – when there was meaningful resistance Soviet casualties were sometimes far from trivial. According to one count of Soviet casualties during the 'liberation' of Western Belorussia and the Ukraine, Soviet forces lost 852 killed or died during casualty evacuation, 144 missing and 2,002 wounded during active operations. [RASWW, p.129] The tank behind the soldiers in the picture is an early model T-26 (Model 1932) with two small turrets with a machine gun in each. Of limited value as such tanks were by the start of the Second World War, there were still more than 1,000 of them in service with the Red Army at the beginning of April 1941 out of more than 1,600 manufactured.[5]

(*Opposite, above*) Sputnik 432037. This photograph in many ways highlights the complex inter-national situation in Eastern Europe in late 1939. Here Soviet troops are shown on the streets of Wilno – later Vilnius – apparently on 20 September 1939. At this time Wilno was part of Poland, having been effectively seized by Polish forces from the fledgling independent Lithuanian state in 1920. By the end of October 1939 the city would be handed over to Lithuanian control by Soviet forces, after Lithuania had 'invited' Soviet troops into the country that month under the auspices of a mutual assistance treaty imposed on it by the Soviet Union. At the end of the summer of 1940 the Soviet Union would compel Lithuania to join the Soviet Union as the Lithuanian Soviet Socialist Republic. The territories of the Baltic Republics were soon to be militarised by the Red Army as airfields and other military infrastructure was hurriedly constructed. Whether the Baltic Republics were intended as forward defensive positions for the Soviet Union or as a springboard for offensive operations westwards was to depend on circumstances. Any intention that the Baltic Republics would serve the latter function would, however, be quashed by Nazi Germany.

(*Left*) Sputnik 494034. This final photo relating to the Soviet invasion of Poland is dated 3 November 1939, and the caption reads 'a peasant tells a Red Army lieutenant of the location of a hostile element during the period of the liberation of Western Belorussia'. This combination of caption and date certainly suggests that the Red Army troops in the photo are engaged in the suppression of real or perceived opposition to Soviet rule after Polish territory had been formally incorporated into the Soviet Union. The lieutenant is still wearing a *Budenovka* hat, first introduced during the Russian Civil War. Such hats continued to be worn into the early period of the Great Patriotic War.

Sputnik 45612. Nazi Germany received considerable quantities of raw materials from the Soviet Union after the signing of the Nazi-Soviet Pact and associated economic agreements. Here, at Peremishl', a Soviet official signs over a shipment of oil to his German counterparts in February 1940. The fact that Nazi Germany was receiving such shipments right up until the German invasion of June 1941 was seen by Stalin as one of the reasons why Hitler would not actually order an invasion of the Soviet Union. That Hitler did just that – and despite the continued state of war between Nazi Germany and Britain – highlighted the extent to which ideology rather than pragmatism was informing German decision-making.

(*Above*) Sputnik 45604. A Soviet 203mm B-4 gun fires on Finnish positions in late 1939. Finnish forces could not hope to compete with the Red Army in terms of firepower, and such super-heavy Soviet artillery was used with some success to reduce Finnish fortifications, and particularly those of the so-called Mannerheim defence line. Soviet artillery was particularly potent when fired over open sights – that is when the crew could see the target – rather than being fired indirectly. Indirect fire required not only far greater training, but also the communications equipment for observers to relay instructions to the guns. During the Great Patriotic War Soviet forces would continue to use artillery in a direct-fire role far more frequently than their opponents or allies.

(*Overleaf*) Sputnik 45601. Soviet scouts receive instructions from a commander sometime in late 1939 on Finnish territory. Take note of their clothing – a far cry from the white camouflage smocks that are iconic for Soviet forces operating in winter during the Great Patriotic War. A reconnaissance soldier of the 17th Independent Ski Battalion operating against the Finns retrospectively recalled what he thought about the suitability of his equipment for his scouting role, writing: 'What sort of Scouts are we!?' – 'we are asses or camels loaded up and unable to turn around … Our kit hampered us – we were neither manoeuvrable nor particularly mobile and operating in biting frost and deep snow!'[RASWW, p. 142] At least some of their Finnish opponents were far better equipped for operating away from the roads in the deep snow of the forest. In early January 1940 one Soviet staff officer noted that Red Army troops were all too often 'frightened by the forest and cannot ski', with some of the troops committed in Finland having being transferred from areas of the Soviet Union that did not offer similar conditions to those being experienced in Finland in winter. [RASWW, p. 145]

(*Below*) Sputnik 40453. These Red Army snipers – also pictured in late 1939 – are better equipped for the conditions than the scouts pictured in the previous photograph. After the débâcle of the early phase of the war in Finland – when such clothing was in short supply – the Red Army would make great efforts to be better equipped for winter warfare in the future, be that in terms of having the right clothing available, to actually training in winter conditions rather than solely during the summer. It was Finnish snipers – or 'cuckoos' as they were known to Soviet troops – who would develop a fearsome reputation during the Soviet war against Finland that would contribute to the Soviet penchant for sniping during the Great Patriotic War.

Sputnik 60383. Another area in which the Red Army would become much more capable during the Great Patriotic War was in conducting river crossings. Here Red Army forces have bridged a river in Karelia at the very end of 1939. The absence of specialised bridging equipment is very much evident, with the large number of vehicles backed up on the 'friendly' side of the river suggesting that getting across the river was a slow process. Few Soviet vehicles at this time were four- or all-wheel drive, further hampering the Soviet advance.

Sputnik 5658622. Soviet horse artillery on the move in Finland in late 1939. Soviet forces in Finland were very much road-bound thanks to the terrain, few four- or all-wheel drive vehicles, and a mindset that limited the willingness of Soviet commanders to move away from the few roads that were available. Long and slow-moving Soviet columns were very vulnerable to attack by Finnish forces from the flanks, with many Soviet troops perishing in the withering cold after they had been isolated from their comrades by Finnish troops.

Sputnik 5659460. A photo very much capturing the cold of the so-called Winter War. Here Red Army soldiers are wearing *Budenovka* hats and great coats in Finland in late 1939. Looking little different than some of their predecessors during the Russian Civil War, they would suffer and die in Finland by the tens of thousands at the hands of both the Finns and the cold.

(*Above*) Sputnik 872655. Here a Soviet T-28 tank is shown in Finland later in the war in early February 1940, by which point the Red Army was starting to get its house in order. Not only were the infantry starting to use far more appropriate small unit tactics against fortified Finnish positions, but the Red Army was deploying tanks with some effect where Finnish ranged anti-tank weapons were few. The Soviet Union had developed a number of multi-turreted tanks during the 1930s, with the T-28 being the most numerous. Although on paper they seemed a good idea, in practice these multi-turreted tanks were not only unwieldy in terms of size, but could not be provided with strong armour if they were not to become even less mobile than they already were. Co-ordination of the fire of multiple turrets was also something that in practice proved extremely difficult for an overtaxed tank commander, and the multi-turreted tank concept was finally abandoned by the Red Army after the war in Finland. The bulk of Soviet stocks of such tanks were expended during the first days of the Great Patriotic War.

(*Overleaf*) Sputnik 54203. Here Soviet forces enter Riga in June 1940. Although Soviet troops had been based in the Baltic Republics since the autumn of 1939, a full Soviet occupation of the Baltic Republics did not take place until the following summer, after the defeat of Anglo-French forces in France. During the same period Soviet forces would also occupy Bessarabia further south. After Soviet forces moved into the Baltic Republics the Red Army would have to expend considerable resources in developing the infrastructure for the basing of troops that previously had been based further east. The development of this infrastructure and indeed fortifications along the border with Nazi Germany was far from complete when Axis forces launched Operation Barbarossa – the invasion of the Soviet Union – on 22 June 1941.

(*Below*) Sputnik 61676. Although taking place in late August 1941, this photo of Soviet troops entering Tabriz in Iran is included in this chapter for the sake of coherence given that this chapter has Soviet pre-war or in this case early-war expansion as a theme. Britain and the Soviet Union jointly invaded Iran at the beginning of the Great Patriotic War, and in doing so secured for the Allies what would become an important conduit for Western Allied assistance to the Soviet Union during the second half of the Second World War. Soviet and British troops would pull out of Iran in 1946. Note how the soldiers pictured here are equipped with the helmet that would be used by the bulk of Soviet troops during the Great Patriotic War, the then new Model 1939/1940 helmet.

Chapter 4

'Barbarossa'

Despite preparations for future war that had lasted more than a decade, and specifically from 1936 for a war against Nazi Germany, the Soviet Union was caught off guard by the Axis invasion of 22 June 1941 – codenamed 'Barbarossa'. Regardless of whether Soviet intentions were purely defensive, or Soviet military expansion and reorganisation was geared towards offensive operations westwards at some point in the future, the Red Army was not ready to fight in June 1941. Stalin had certainly convinced himself to at least some extent that Hitler would be foolish to attack the Soviet Union that summer, although Soviet forces had nonetheless massed in the border regions, for what purpose remains unclear. That a significant proportion of the Soviet Union's vast mechanised forces were concentrated along the Soviet border with Nazi Germany and her allies – with divisions in many instances only partially manned and with insufficient supplies – put them in a very vulnerable position that German forces would quickly exploit. Very few contemporary Soviet photos exist of those mechanised forces that summer that would fight some of the largest tank battles in history in the Ukraine, in part because their defeat was so complete. Ordered to counter-attack against the advancing Axis forces rather than attempting some sort of orderly retreat, the Red Army lost not only thousands of tanks and other pieces of equipment, but millions of soldiers caught in vast German encirclements that would take Axis forces weeks to fully reduce. Nonetheless, the Red Army that fought the Axis advance that summer was undoubtedly tactically at least more capable than it would have been had Soviet forces gone to war back in 1938 or 1939, and was starting to receive an increasing amount of new equipment that would be the match or superior to even the latest German equivalents – the T-34 tank being the iconic example. Behind those Soviet forces destroyed in the border regions lay a second echelon, soon to be joined by fresh if often poorly trained and equipped units that were the result of a full mobilisation of the Red Army and the creation of new units. The hundreds of thousands who would be killed or taken prisoner only to die in German camps were in many ways lives squandered, but at the same time they exacted a steady toll on advancing Axis forces that would gradually contribute to a degradation of Axis combat capabilities. At a cost of hundreds of thousands of lives, Hitler's plans to defeat the Soviet Union in a single crushing blow that summer were thwarted.

The Axis on the offensive – the Great Patriotic War from 22 June 1941 to 19 November 1942.

Sputnik 62161. The first photo in the first chapter of those dealing with the Great Patriotic War is perhaps surprisingly of a German: Alfred Liskow. Liskow – a German communist born in Kolberg in 1910 – would during the evening of 21 June 1941 desert from his unit and swim across the Bug river to Soviet positions and inform his captors of the German invasion to come that forthcoming morning. By the time his testimony had been pushed up the Soviet chain of command, the wheels of a Soviet response to the imminent threat of invasion were starting to turn as Soviet forces were all too late put on a higher state of alert. Many Soviet units would not receive these orders before the first German bombs fell and German forces launched themselves eastwards. Despite his heroism, Liskow's fate in Soviet hands is uncertain. Although used as a willing propaganda tool by the Soviet side – with this photograph appearing in the Soviet press – it seems that his critical stance over the activities of the Soviet-sponsored Communist International or Comintern prior to the war might have played a role in the fact that he did not survive to see the defeat of Nazi Germany.

Sputnik 2172. Some of the Soviet wounded of the first days of the war make their way back from the front line. Although it is unclear where and exactly when this picture was taken, it no doubt shows a typical scene being repeated across the front. If lucky, these two soldiers were able to escape the encirclements that would see so many of their compatriots end up in German PoW camps, and in which they would all too often not survive the winter of 1941/1942 as a result of wilful neglect.

Sputnik 65718. Another image from the first days of the war, this time by a different photographer, showing a Soviet soldier having his wounds dressed with the assistance of Soviet civilians. This photograph, and the next concerning refugees, gives some sense of the chaos at the front during the first days of the war.

Sputnik 432. A long line of refugees retreats from the fighting on the horizon during the first days of the war, in this case somewhere in the Ukraine. As the summer progressed, Soviet civilians were discouraged from retreating with the Red Army unless their evacuation was a sanctioned part of the relocation of Soviet industry to the east. Such a policy certainly meant that disruption caused to forces moving to the front by refugees moving in the opposite direction was minimised, but at a cost. As a result of such a policy a peak of more than 70 million Soviet citizens would find themselves living on Axis-occupied territory. Those who were able would be expected to join or assist the Communist underground or Soviet partisan units operating near where they lived. As shown in Chapter 9, many did join the partisans, and many lost their lives not only resisting foreign occupation but also in German and Axis retribution against the civilian population for the activities of the underground and partisans nearby or as part of the Final Solution to the Jewish Question – the Holocaust.

(*Above*) Sputnik 662757. New recruits for the Red Army in Moscow on 23 June 1941. Although the Axis invasion prompted a full mobilisation and successive waves of conscription into the Red Army, at the beginning of the war in the cities in particular there was no shortage of volunteers for the Red Army. Although keen to harness this initial enthusiasm to defend the Motherland, the authorities did, however, have to make sure not to allow the volunteering of skilled workers to denude the factories of personnel who were likely to be of greater service in the rear. Sadly many volunteers would be thrown into action with only limited training as the Red Army's need for replacements took precedence over desirable training regimens.

(*Opposite, above*) Sputnik 594348. This second picture of new recruits for the Red Army was taken on 24 June in Moscow, and shows them being provided with their uniforms. The scale of Soviet losses during the summer and autumn of 1941, combined with stocks lost to the enemy and damage done to production by the war, would mean that many items of clothing for the Red Army would soon be in relatively short supply. Long boots as shown here that used a lot of leather would soon no longer be available for distribution to mere rank-and-file conscripts. As the war progressed the Western Allies would provide many millions of pairs of boots for the Red Army.

(*Opposite, below*) Sputnik 662733. In this picture, also taken on 23 June, recently mobilised Red Army troops are shown heading towards the front. Note that they are equipped with both the Model 1936 and Model 1939/1940 helmets. The sign on the left reads, 'Our task is righteous, the enemy will be crushed, victory will be ours!' This is a quote from the end of Soviet foreign minister Viacheslav Molotov's address to the Soviet people of the previous day, announcing the beginning of the war. [See GPW, p. 43 for the introduction to this speech] That Stalin didn't make that speech was no doubt noted by some, and contributed to the notion in some Western Cold War-era literature on the war that Stalin was somehow incapacitated at the beginning of the war. Stalin was indeed briefly incapacitated at the very end of the month after he had become aware of the capture of the Belorussian capital Minsk by German forces and the poor state of the forces of the Western Front on the key Moscow axis. However, the evidence available suggests that Stalin had soon recovered from his apparently short-lived depressive state in good time in order to give his first speech of the war to the Soviet people on 3 July. [See GPW, pp. 49–50].

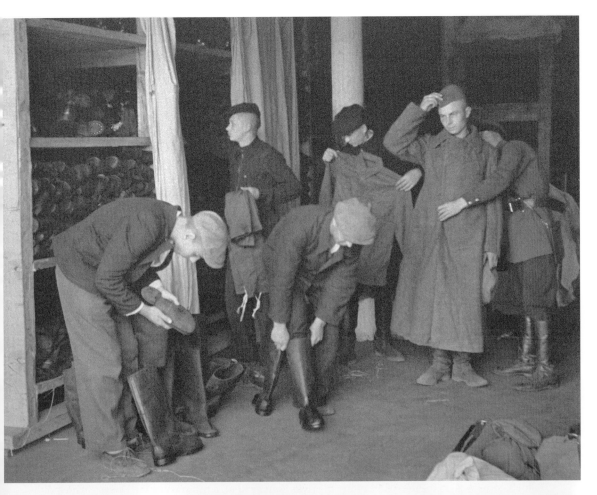

НАШЕ ДЕЛО ПРАВОЕ.
ВРАГ БУДЕТ РАЗБИТ.
ПОБЕДА БУДЕТ
ЗА НАМИ!

Sputnik 601169. BA-10 armoured cars near the Romanian border early in the war. The Axis advance in the south began after that in the centre and north, giving Soviet forces in the region a chance to prepare for combat. Consequently the Axis advance was slower in the south, creating a situation where Axis forces in the centre were soon significantly further east than those in the south. A halt of the Axis advance in the centre and transfer of resources to north and south helped the Soviets achieve a rare operational success in the summer of 1941 in the centre at El'nia in early September.

Sputnik 2517. A cavalry unit of Pavel Belov's 2nd Cavalry Corps near Tiraspol' in Moldavia on 11 July 1941. According to the war diary for what would become the 1st Guards Cavalry Corps, Belov's corps was on the defensive along the river Raut or Reut, a tributary of the Dnestr.[6] Tiraspol' was on Romanian territory prior to Bessarabia being ceded to the Soviet Union in June 1940. In early August the city was occupied by Romanian troops fighting as part of the Axis, and was then incorporated into Transnistria. In the foreground a Maxim machine gun is mounted on a horse-drawn carriage, together known as a *tachanka*. The crew appear to be watching for aircraft, at a time when the Luftwaffe typically had air superiority over the battlefield.

Sputnik 612. Taken on 5 August 1941, this photograph shows a Soviet sailor chatting with an Odessan militiaman prior to the point at which the port of Odessa was encircled on its landward sides by Axis forces. In many Soviet cities threatened by Axis forces such workers' militia were hastily organised and thrown into their defence alongside the Red Army. Although many Soviet citizens had either served in the Red Army or had some sort of pre-conscription military training, such militia units were no substitute for regular Red Army units.

Sputnik 59232. This very evocative picture shows Red Army soldiers in action somewhere near Odessa after it had been encircled on its landward sides by Axis forces but before it had been captured by the enemy. The siege of Odessa would in fact last from early August until mid-October 1941, with Soviet naval forces initially bringing in troops and supplies by sea and later evacuating them as the prospects of holding out deteriorated.

Sputnik 6046555. A third picture taken near Odessa in late August 1941 showing sailors hitching a ride on a 'Komsomolets' artillery tractor. Such tractors had been produced prior to the war with the intention of providing the Red Army's light artillery – including anti-tank guns – with a motorised means to more rapidly deploy than if they were towed by horses. In all, 7,780 were manufactured between 1937 and 1941.[7] Most 'Komsomolets' tractors were lost during 1941 and not replaced as Soviet industry focused its productive effort on the production of tanks. Such light armoured tractors would be largely replaced in the towing role with either lorries of either Soviet or US manufacture, or other vehicles supplied under Lend-Lease. Sailors were frequently called on to fight on land during the Great Patriotic War, with substantial numbers not only participating in the defence of such port cities as Odessa and Leningrad, but also participating in the fighting further inland for cities such as Stalingrad.

Sputnik 76. The official caption for this photograph reads 'Soldiers of one of the units of the 20th Army (Western Front) engaged in battle on the banks of the Dnepr River, west of Dorogobuzh.' Dorogobuzh is in the Smolensk region, the scene of prolonged and intense fighting. The historic town of Dorogobuzh was almost equidistant between Smolensk and Viaz'ma on the key Moscow axis – the former captured by German forces on 16 July, the latter associated with of one of the major German encirclements of Soviet forces in October 1941, during operations that will be considered in Chapter 5. To the south of Dorogobuzh was the town of El'nia, briefly liberated by Soviet forces in early September only to be recaptured by German forces at the beginning of the following month. The troops shown here were quite possibly involved in those early September Soviet offensive operations. Dorogobuzh would fall to the Wehrmacht very early on during renewed German offensive operations in early October, and the 20th Army was subsequently caught in the Viaz'ma encirclement – the second time it had been encircled that summer. The troops in the picture are clearly in rather pristine uniforms, suggesting that they were relatively fresh troops and even that this was perhaps their first taste of combat. Note also their lack of helmets – not unusual during this period of the war and something that was relatively typical for Soviet forces throughout the war. Whilst at times there were shortages of helmets, even when they were available some Soviet troops chose not to wear them for reasons of comfort. Without a helmet such troops were of course at a significantly greater risk of suffering often fatal head injuries due to shrapnel in particular.

Sputnik 1228. Red Army troops are once again shown in action here in September 1941 in the Smolensk region. The official caption notes that they are shown in action fighting for heights on the right bank of the Dnepr river. As in the previous photo, they appear to be relatively fresh troops, and are similarly not wearing helmets. Note the commander on the left who does not have a rifle – making it plain to German snipers and other combatants that he is an officer. The Red Army – as many other armies – would as the war progressed move away from allowing junior officers to single themselves out in such a fashion.

Sputnik 2066. The artillery piece shown here is in action in early September 1941 somewhere close to the dam of the Dnepr Hydroelectric Station constructed during the first of the Soviet Union's Five-Year Plans in southern Ukraine, at what had been Aleksandrovsk, later Zaporizhia. The gun shown is a relatively modern piece for the time: an M-10 Model 1938 122mm Howitzer. Such artillery pieces, of which well over 3,000 had been produced by the end of 1941 alone, would serve throughout the Great Patriotic War. Some of the examples captured by German forces were used to make up German artillery units. It is quite possible that such was the fate of this particular weapon.

Chapter 5

On the Moscow Axis

By the end of September 1941 Axis forces – primarily German – had destroyed much of the Red Army that had existed in June 1941. By the end of what in Soviet terms was known as 'The Kiev Strategic Defensive Operation' that ran from 7 July through to 26 September 1941, the Red Army had lost more than 600,000 troops as 'irrecoverable losses' in the Ukraine, with the South-Western Front alone losing more than 500,000. [RASWW, p. 247] 'Irrecoverable losses' were, as the term suggests, those losses which the Red Army could not reasonably expect to get back, meaning not only those killed, but also those missing and taken prisoner by the enemy. Of the more than 600,000 troops lost in the Kiev region in an encirclement of epic proportions, the vast majority were lost as prisoners of war. However, although Axis forces had captured much of the western part of the Soviet Union as well, they had not destroyed the Soviet ability to create and equip new units – as well as transfer units from the Far East that had been guarding against the possibility of further Japanese aggression in the region.

During the pause in the German advance on the key central axis towards Moscow in the late summer of 1941, the Soviet Union managed to throw fresh forces into the distant defence of the capital. When the German advance on Moscow resumed in earnest on 2 October 1941 these troops would ensure that the German advance would be fiercely, if not necessarily coherently, resisted. Soon, as the previous month near Kiev, hundreds of thousands of Soviet troops would be encircled in pockets of resistance near Briansk and Viaz'ma as German forces showed their operational superiority. German successes on the Moscow axis would see a state of siege declared for Moscow on 16 October, with plans being made for the evacuation of the Soviet government to the east. However, operational superiority alone would not win the war for Germany as often stubborn Soviet resistance, fatigue, both losses of and wear-and-tear on equipment, and issues with extended supply lines across territory not cleared of roving bands of Red Army personnel cut off from their lines took their toll on German forces. All of these factors would prove an impediment to the German advance even without the onset of the rainy season in the autumn, that would see the German advance literally bogged down in the face of mud and Soviet resistance by the end of October. By the time the German advance on Moscow could be resumed in earnest in early November the Red Army had once again been able to throw new units in front of German forces. By the end of November increasingly small German spearheads sought to punch through to the Soviet capital but to no avail, as the Red Army found the strength to launch local counter-attacks that would soon snowball into a major counter-offensive. The German Blitzkrieg had been halted, and the much-vaunted Wehrmacht would be thrown back from the gates of the Soviet capital. This chapter examines the Soviet defence of Moscow from the start of renewed German offensive operations towards Moscow at the beginning of October 1941 – Operation 'Typhoon' – to the weekend of 5–7 December when localised Soviet counter-attacks became something much more significant.

(*Below*) Sputnik 77. Red Army troops of an undisclosed unit defend a bridge from dug-in positions sometime around the very beginning of October 1941 in the Smolensk region. These quite possibly fresh troops would soon find themselves in the maelstrom of battle as German mechanised forces punched through Soviet lines and raced eastwards, leaving the infantry to 'mop up' often encircled Soviet forces left in their wake. Clearly at the point that this photograph was taken the weather had not yet taken a turn for the worse – although the temperature had clearly dropped from the summer the leaves were still on many trees and the first snows had yet to fall.

(*Opposite, above*) Sputnik 2551. Less than two weeks later than in the previous photograph and the weather had clearly shifted, bringing the first snow to the battlefields on the Moscow axis. This photograph is dated 10 October, and shows Soviet tanks moving up to the front through a village somewhere in the Moscow region. Both tanks are T-26s – the lead tank a later model and the second tank an earlier one. Note the whitewash applied to the tanks as camouflage in the new weather conditions. During this period of the fighting on the Moscow axis the Red Army would throw almost any tanks it had available into the fray in a desperate attempt to halt German forces on defence lines that had been constructed to protect Moscow.

(*Opposite, below*) Sputnik 3500. Muscovites involved in the construction of a defensive line somewhere outside Moscow during October 1941. Thousands of civilians were mobilised to construct the series of defensive lines for the protection of the capital in what was not only arduous work, but work also made more onerous by the deteriorating weather conditions. Note that both men and women alike are involved in digging these positions.

Sputnik 616433. This is a relatively rare photograph in that it shows Soviet motorcycle troops early in the war, in this case on 16 October somewhere in the Moscow region. Both German and Soviet forces – but particularly the former – would make use of the motorcycle in a reconnaissance role early in the war. Later in the war the use of the motorcycle in this role was not as frequent for German forces, with armoured cars and other armoured vehicles being preferred, in part because of the greater protection from the enemy that they offered. Soviet use of the motorcycle seems actually to have increased by the mid-war period. By the date this photograph was taken German forces had breached the Mozhaisk line defending Moscow – about halfway between the city and Viaz'ma – and the evacuation of the Soviet capital had been set in motion the previous day.

Sputnik 601158. Although this picture might be confused with pictures showing the famous parade held in Moscow on 7 November 1941 to celebrate the anniversary of the Russian Revolution, it was in fact apparently taken on 23 October. It shows Soviet artillery on its way to the front through the streets of Moscow. Of note are the older artillery pieces being towed by lorries: it was not only older tanks but also other equipment that would be thrown into action in defence of Moscow. Note that the guns have wooden-spoked wheels, which would reduce the speed they could be safely towed to little more than a fast march.

Sputnik 604269. Although taken during the summer of 1941, this photograph was selected because it so effectively symbolises Moscow and indeed the Soviet Union at war. Clearly shown in the background is the Kremlin in all its glory, pictured underneath threatening clouds. The anti-aircraft gun in the foreground is being crewed by both men and women. During the period with which this chapter is concerned Moscow would come under frequent air attack.

(*Opposite, above*) Sputnik 279. The German assault on Moscow in the autumn of 1941 saw two German pincers seek to encircle the Soviet capital from the north-east and south. The defence of the south hinged to a large extent on the defence of the town of Tula. Early in the war Soviet forces had made little use of built-up areas for defence, but were soon ordered to do so more frequently. Whilst defending urban areas meant that the civilian population would suffer more from the ravages of war in their locale, the defence of urban areas sapped German strength and proved to be a great leveller in combat between the Red Army and the Wehrmacht. Here an anti-aircraft gun is being used in a ground defence role somewhere in what are probably the outskirts of Tula at the end of November 1941.

(*Opposite, below*) Sputnik 2558. Here Soviet troops are shown dug-in covering a street close to the centre of Tula on the same day as Sputnik 279 above. The soldier on the right is armed with an anti-tank rifle – a weapon used by the Red Army well into the Great Patriotic War even as other armies had all but abandoned the concept. Soviet anti-tank rifles were more effective than shorter versions in service with other armies, but were still unable to penetrate the armour of increasingly well protected tanks. Such anti-tank rifles did continue to have value against lighter armoured vehicles, and were also used at times for sniping – including against aircraft!

(*Above*) Sputnik 5686100. Soviet enthusiasm for the anti-tank rifle is well illustrated in this picture of a tank destruction unit pictured somewhere on Russian territory during November 1941. To some extent the PTRD anti-tank rifle was used to make up for insufficient anti-tank guns in Soviet rifle divisions in late 1941, although they were a poor substitute.

(*Left*) Sputnik 431876. A poster by Soviet artist Boris Mukhin simply stating 'We will defend [our] native Moscow!', with the text accompanied by a soldier, a militiaman, a sailor and a woman serving in an unconfirmed role in defence of Moscow. There were in fact relatively few sailors involved in the defence of Moscow, but the poster is in keeping with Soviet propaganda stemming from the Revolution and Civil War in portraying not only different services but also civilians in a militia role, at the time of the Revolution having been known as the Red Guard.

(*Above*) Sputnik 669661. These KV-1 tanks are shown on a street in Moscow just after the famous parade held on 7 November 1941 to celebrate the anniversary of the October Revolution (being celebrated on the appropriate day in the new calendar). The parade in 1941 was notable because it took place when Moscow was officially under siege, and where the Red Army units involved frequently found themselves dispatched to the front line soon after having paraded through Red Square. Holding the parade in such circumstances represented a propaganda coup for Stalin and the Soviet leadership, which would go some way to convincing those at home and abroad that the Soviet Union was not finished. These KV-1 tanks would have been particularly in demand at the front line at this time, representing – along with the T-34 – the best of the Soviet tanks then available. The KV-1 tank was almost impervious to the lighter anti-tank and tank guns then in use with the German Wehrmacht, often requiring the expenditure of considerable resources on the part of German forces for their neutralisation. Most famously these tanks would be stopped by the infamous 88mm German anti-aircraft gun in one of its increasingly numerous guises. Fortunately for the Wehrmacht, production of the KV-1 was only just picking up speed when German forces invaded the Soviet Union, and only 368 of all modifications were on hand as of 1 April 1941.[8]

(*Opposite, above*) Sputnik 390. This photograph once again shows Soviet anti-tank troops armed with anti-tank rifles, also in November 1941. The location in this instance is somewhere near the small town of Zvenigorod to the immediate west of Moscow. This picture is particularly suitable for inclusion here in the sense that it gives a good feel for some of the terrain being fought over in late 1941 on the Moscow axis, where between settlements there were frequent and often sizeable forested areas that often were far from good tank country. The picture also makes it plain that winter conditions hampered the activities of both sides, the icy conditions here making climbing this piece of steeper ground that bit more difficult.

(*Opposite, below*) Sputnik 58848. By late November 1941 it was far more likely than it had been only weeks before that Soviet troops would be fielding captured German equipment against its previous owners, as Soviet troops were by now more frequently getting the better of their German opponents in the increasingly small-scale engagements on the approaches to Moscow. Here one 'Sergeant Zhruravlev' is pictured with his gun crew using a captured 5cm PaK 38 anti-tank gun against German forces. The capture of these guns with ammunition by Soviet crews would have been a boon in late 1941 at a time when the Red Army was short of anti-tank guns.

(*Above*) Sputnik 5822580. This photograph, taken on 20 November 1941, actually shows Soviet troops in action on the streets of Rostov-on-Don in the far south of the Soviet Union rather than near Moscow. It was here, rather than at Moscow, that German forces suffered their first obvious reverse, as they were pushed back from the Caucasus in late November 1941. They would soon also suffer a similar fate not only on the outskirts of Moscow but near Tikhvin, east of Leningrad. Note that the Soviet troops in this picture are still only equipped with rifles, as the sub-machine guns that would become almost ubiquitous in the Red Army were still not available in large numbers. Being equipped only with rifles would put Soviet troops at a disadvantage against German forces in some situations where German troops at least had some MP 40 sub-machine guns for use at relatively close quarters.

(*Opposite*) Sputnik 2549. The final picture in this chapter gives what is in many senses a taste of things to come on a larger scale in Chapter 8: the Red Army on the attack. In this photograph Soviet cavalry are shown on the attack somewhere near Moscow on 2 December 1941. By this time Soviet forces were increasingly frequently engaged in local offensive operations that would soon snowball into a wider offensive near Moscow during the weekend of 5–7 December. Cavalry undoubtedly had a useful role to play over the vast expanses of the Soviet Union and Eastern Europe, and would continue to be employed by the Red Army through to the end of the war. As will be further discussed in Chapter 8, the horse offered considerable mobility to light forces even in winter. Whilst creating a dramatic impression, cavalry charges such as this one were, however, only very rarely effective against any sort of organised opposition – the horse was best left as a means of transport, not of assault. In one particularly egregious instance in mid-November two regiments of the 44th Cavalry Division charged dug-in German troops of the 106th Infantry Division near Musino on the approaches to Klin to the north-east of Moscow. One German observer described some of the cavalry as offering 'an unbelievably beautiful sight on a clear sunny winter landscape' as they went into the attack 'with gleaming sabres above their heads'. The massacre that seems to

have followed was in stark contrast to such words, offering 'a nightmarish performance' for the German soldiers. [RASWW, p. 311] Total losses for the 44th Cavalry Division from 16 November to 21 December 1941 were a horrendous 3,299 men (of whom 405 were reported as killed and 1,624 missing) and 3,595 horses (of which 1,830 were reported as killed and 1,471 missing).[9]

Chapter 6

Leningrad Besieged

During the summer and autumn of 1941 Axis forces destroyed much of the pre-war strength of the Red Army. Millions of Red Army personnel found themselves trapped in multiple instances of encirclement on the Moscow axis, both during the first weeks of the war and in October. In the south the encirclement of mid-September near Kiev ripped the heart out of Soviet forces in that region, not only facilitating the advance of Axis forces towards the Caucasus, but removing a southern threat to the German advance on Moscow. In the north, however, both on the axis of advance towards Leningrad and in the Arctic in the far north, Red Army forces did not suffer the encirclements of their colleagues to the south. On the Leningrad axis the Red Army was pushed back towards what had been the capital prior to the winter of 1918, but in relatively good order by the standards of the summer as a whole. In many ways this is explained by the geography of the region, where the combination of lakes, forest and marshes was not suited to the broad mechanised sweeps possible in the centre and particularly on the open steppe in the south. On the Leningrad axis, having the Baltic Sea as a flank further limited German opportunities for manoeuvre. Nonetheless, despite the Soviet authorities having formed defensive lines to protect Leningrad from the south – and having thrown poorly trained militia units into their defence in a desperate attempt to stem the German advance – by 8 September German forces had reached Lake Ladoga to the east of Leningrad and cut the city's land communications with the remainder of the Soviet Union. With the Finns having reoccupied Karelian territory to the north as part of their 'continuation war' with the Soviet Union, Leningrad was hemmed in and under siege.

Although German plans for the invasion of the Soviet Union – Operation 'Barbarossa' – had slated Leningrad for capture by German forces, after they had reached the outskirts of the city in September 1941 plans changed. Fighting for the city would undoubtedly have proven costly for German forces, and the decision was made instead to lay siege to the city and starve, shell and bomb it into submission before ultimately levelling it. The siege of Leningrad had begun, and would drag on until January 1943 before limited land communications with the Soviet heartland were restored, and January 1944 before the siege could be said to have been fully lifted. During that period more than a million of its inhabitants would die – many of muscle wastage caused by starvation or of illnesses that in other circumstances they might very well have survived. The vast majority of those who died did so during the winter of 1941/1942, during which the deaths of so many made it more feasible to feed the remainder. During this period being a soldier was for once something of a saving grace, since rations for front-line troops were better than for other categories of Leningrad's defenders and inhabitants. For much of the war – as the dramas of the Battles of Moscow, Stalingrad and Kursk were fought elsewhere – Leningrad held out stubbornly, relying to a large extent on its own resources. There were, however, numerous attempts to lift the siege, a number of which failed because they were far too ambitious in their aims and went far beyond trying to simply punch a corridor through to the city. This chapter is concerned with the siege of Leningrad, and illustrates not only events leading up to and the siege itself, but also the eventual relief of the city.

(*Opposite, above left*) Sputnik 715710. This first photo was taken on 29 June 1941, and shows children being evacuated from the city of Leningrad into the rural areas around it. Although at this time the threat to the city from German forces to the south was not acute, Finnish forces were moving towards the city from the north. Leningrad's vulnerability in 1918 when it was Petrograd certainly provided a precedent for seeing it as vulnerable in 1941, and that was at a time when aerial bombing of cities was in its infancy. According to statistics for the city's Evacuation Commission, from 29 June to 27 August 395,091 children were evacuated from the city, but because of enemy action 175,400 were returned to Leningrad. Additionally during the same period 164,320 'workers and administrative personnel' were evacuated, along with industrial concerns that were relocated to safer areas to the east, as well as an additional 104,691 residents. Although this meant that 488,703 had been evacuated from the city, 147,500 were evacuated to Leningrad from the Soviet Baltic Republics and Karelia. [GPW, pp. 150–1] Subsequently some of those from within Leningrad were evacuated by boat or by air before Lake Ladoga had frozen over, or across the ice road that during the winter months linked Leningrad to Soviet-controlled territory.

(*Opposite, above right*) Sputnik 802. With the city cut off from the remainder of Soviet territory, Soviet soldiers of the 115th Rifle Division are pictured here awaiting an enemy counter-attack after they had secured positions on the left bank of the Neva river near Leningrad during the latter half of September 1941. The division had previously been based in Karelia, but had been pushed back on Leningrad by the Finns. With the division reinforced, two battalions of the division then took part in operations to seize a bridgehead over the Neva river to the south-east of the city during the night of 19/20 September 1941. During 6–7 October the remainder of the division was transferred across the Neva to participate in fighting on the bridgehead that would see the division take heavy losses. A printed version of the division's history for the first year of the war makes specific note of the poor rations available to its troops during this period given the food situation in Leningrad, and of the 'exhaustion and physical weakness of soldiers and commanders who had just left Leningrad hospitals'.[10]

(*Opposite, below*) Sputnik 770. Soviet militia are shown here in action somewhere on the outskirts of Leningrad during October 1941, after the city had been encircled by enemy forces. At this time Stalin clearly did not expect that the siege would last as long as it eventually would. General Zhukov had been given command of the Leningrad Front in early September, but by the point this photograph was taken had probably headed back to the Moscow region to take command of what would become the Western Front there. Such militia units were hastily thrown into action both near Moscow and Leningrad, where they took heavy losses. Militia divisions lacked not only some of the training and equipment afforded to regular divisions, but also the same level of support from artillery and other units. In addition to their rifles, these militiamen do at least seem to have a hand grenade each, placed on the ground in front of them ready to be used to repel an enemy attack.

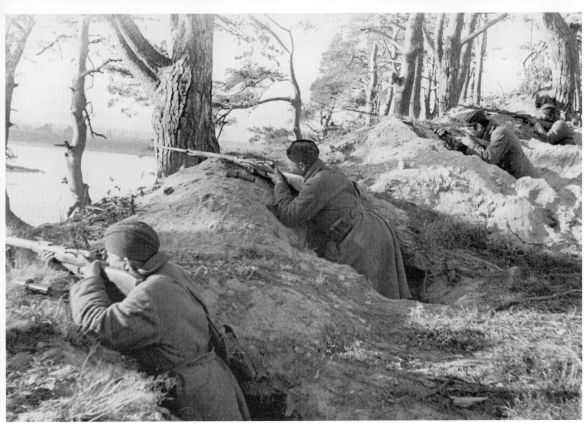

(*Above*) Sputnik 323. Soviet sailors of the Baltic Fleet on their way to the front, also sometime during October 1941. By this point, with the city encircled, their ships were bottled up in the Gulf of Finland with little to do than provide fire-support for ground forces with their guns. Such fire-support did not require all of their crews, meaning that many of the sailors could be sent to the front as ground troops. Their footwear is far from ideal for ground forces, and they also lack helmets and greatcoats.

(*Opposite, above*) Sputnik 637272. In many ways better provided for are these Soviet reinforcements heading towards the front in late October 1941. They are photographed here not far from the famous Winter Palace in the centre of Leningrad, marching past the former Tsarist Admiralty building. Note once again the absence of helmets, and the fact that they are all armed only with rifles – typical for this period of the war. It is unclear whether these soldiers are part of a militia or a regular army unit.

(*Opposite, below*) Sputnik 286. Soviet troops with a camouflaged F-22 (76.2mm Divisional Gun Model 1936) divisional artillery piece sometime in early November 1941 during the 2nd Siniavino Operation – one of many attempts to lift the siege of Leningrad. Although the snow on the ground suggests colder temperatures, the churned-up road is testimony to how bad conditions could get for the mobility of either side during the autumn. The slightly higher temperatures near Leningrad would mean that such conditions were more likely to last longer on that sector of the front than near Moscow. The F-22 gun in this picture entered service in 1936 as a modernised version of an earlier model, with the Red Army receiving 2,932 of these guns by the end of 1939. Most of these guns were either destroyed or captured during the fighting in 1941, making their presence in a photograph one indicator of its date. German forces would use some of these guns on tank destroyers where into 1942 German forces faced a shortage of guns with ballistic characteristics sufficient to deal with the armour of the KV-series and T-34 tanks.

(*Opposite, above*) Sputnik 60024. Although many sailors of the Baltic Fleet were sent as infantry to the front line of the ground war, some at least were required to man their ships' guns so that they could operate in support of ground forces in the defence of Leningrad. In the event of German forces looking likely to seize the city, plans had been made to scuttle the Baltic Fleet. Here the destroyer *Opitnii* is shown at her mooring in Leningrad providing fire-support to the Red Army in February 1942. Given that her 'main armament' was reportedly removed from the ship at this time, we can assume that she lacks her forward gun mount, which would explain why pictures of her during this period only show her rear guns that were pointing in the right direction for her to provide fire-support from her berth! This particular vessel was the first in a class that never went into series production, and in fact this ship entered service and left it as a floating battery.[11]

(*Opposite, below*) Sputnik 666681. The aircraft in the foreground of this photograph is an I-16 fighter of the 7th Fighter Air Corps of the Soviet Air Defence forces (PVO) shown in October 1941. In the background Li-2 transport aircraft – originally given the designation PS-84, but in both cases a Soviet-manufactured DC-3 'Dakota' – take off. These aircraft were used in increasing numbers to fly people and supplies in and out of the city, and were particularly valuable during the period when Lake Ladoga was icing up and hence was not navigable by boats, but when the ice wasn't yet solid enough for vehicles to drive on. The German Luftwaffe of course attempted to interdict this supply route into the city, meaning that fighter aircraft such as that pictured here had to be allocated for the defence of the air corridor.

(*Above*) Sputnik 62127. This next photograph shows Li-2 aircraft flying over Lake Ladoga in March 1942. The official caption for this photograph suggests that the aircraft were carrying food, which was indeed one of the categories of goods being flown into the city. Throughout the year these flights allowed food and other key items to be brought into the city quickly. In an order by the Soviet State Defence Committee – the highest organ of Soviet government during the war – of 20 September 1941, a list of items to be flown into the city included fuses for shells, parts in short supply for military vehicles, communications equipment and precious metals for production purposes. [GPW, p. 145]

Sputnik 324. This bleak picture shows a street in Leningrad in April 1942. The couple in the foreground are, according to the official caption, delivering the body of a relative to the cemetery. By this point the death rate in the city was slowing, in part because the available food now had to feed fewer people, given how many tens of thousands had died over the winter. In total, Soviet sources suggest that more than a million deaths in Leningrad during the siege were attributable to starvation, malnutrition and resultant illnesses, enemy activity and other causes relating to the siege – that is, deaths that would not or might not have happened were it not for the siege.

Sputnik 58262. Soviet troops fire flamethrowers in the Leningrad region in September 1942. The Red Army had dedicated units equipped with flamethrowers even during the first year of the war, such as the flamethrower company that was part of a unit formed to destroy German forces in the Kaluga area near Moscow and liberate the town at the end of 1941. [RASWW, p. 312] The Soviets tended to concentrate weapons types in particular units, as illustrated by the antitank rifles in Sputnik 5686100 in Chapter 5 (see p. 61). This certainly simplified resupply.

Sputnik 741. Here Soviet troops are shown with what the official caption suggests is a captured German howitzer near Leningrad during mid-1943. The howitzer in the picture seems, however, to be a 305mm Howitzer Model 1939 of Soviet production, suggesting that it may have been first captured by German forces from the Red Army. Such weapons were a feature of the siege of Leningrad, with German forces employing significant artillery assets in order to 'reduce' the city. The Soviet side responded with its own artillery assets, which of course included the heavy artillery on the ships of the Baltic Fleet.

(*Above*) Sputnik 5635. Pictured here are SU-122 self-propelled guns near the Narva Triumphal Arch in Leningrad sometime during the mid-war period. The arch was constructed to celebrate the Russian victory over Napoleon in 1814. Given that these self-propelled guns were not produced in Leningrad, it is quite probable that they found their way into the city via the corridor punched through along the southern shore of Lake Ladoga during January 1943. Although the Soviet Union had experimented with self-propelled guns prior to the war, it was really the German StuG III self-propelled gun that highlighted their utility when considering the labour and other inputs required to build them compared to a tank, as well as their low profiles and the possibility of adding additional armour where there wasn't the weight of a turret to contend with. These SU-122 guns were produced in late 1942 and early 1943 on the T-34 chassis, before being replaced in production by superior self-propelled guns for the remainder of the war.

(*Opposite, above*) Sputnik 602168. This photograph once again shows Soviet sailors being readied for the front line near Leningrad, but in this case in 1943 on the island of Kronstadt off the city. As is apparent here, later in the war Soviet sailors were being provided with Red Army uniforms and equipment for service as ground troops, rather than going into action in their rather unsuitable naval uniforms. The unit here is apparently the 260th Naval Infantry Brigade, with the picture taken in November 1943.

(*Opposite, below*) Sputnik 448. Although a narrow land corridor had been punched through to Leningrad from the remainder of Soviet territory in January 1943, this corridor was still subject to German artillery bombardment. Soviet sources tend to see the final end to the blockade as having been in January–February 1944, when most of the Leningrad region was liberated from Axis forces. Here Soviet infantry dismount from now aged BA-10 armoured cars at Krasnoe Selo near Leningrad on 19 January 1944. Just as German forces had been unable to encircle large numbers of Soviet troops in the region as they advanced on Leningrad, so Soviet forces were unable to do the same thing as they liberated the region.

Chapter 7

The Soviet Navy at War

As noted in the previous chapter, the Soviet navy's Baltic Fleet was bottled up in Leningrad for much of the war – this after having taken heavy losses as it retreated from forward bases in the Baltic Republics, with the retreat from Tallinn in late August 1941 being a particular débâcle. In the south, the second largest Soviet naval force, the Black Sea Fleet, also suffered heavy losses during the early phases of the war as it too was pushed back from forward bases such as Odessa and its principal base at Sevastopol' all the way to the Caucasus region. Although the Soviet navy had a significant force of cruisers and antiquated battleships, there were no dramatic encounters between Soviet and German capital ships off any of the Soviet coastlines. Because of this, and the fact that the principal fighting was clearly taking place on land, the Soviet navy has often been all but dismissed in Western histories of the Great Patriotic War. To dismiss the Soviet navy to the extent to which is the case in so many Western histories is, however, to ignore the fact that significant elements of the Soviet naval forces saw considerable action during the war not only during retreats in the face of the German and Axis advance, but also in support of the war on land. In the far north, where the Soviet Northern Fleet was not bottled up in its ports, vessels of the Northern Fleet saw action not only in the defence of Allied convoys to the Soviet Union, but also in landing operations against the German coastal flanks. In the Black Sea the retreat from Odessa and Sevastopol' was a protracted affair that saw vessels of the Black Sea Fleet provide significant support to ground forces and the besieged port cities, as well as support for substantial landing operations in the Crimea. Significant Soviet naval forces were also employed on the navigable rivers of the Soviet Union and Eastern Europe, where their contribution to the Axis defeat did not make headlines, but was nonetheless meaningful. Even in the Baltic, towards the end of the war the Baltic Fleet was able to gain some freedom of movement in order to both support Red Army operations on land and interdict German seaborne communications between pockets in the Baltic region and the shrinking heartland of the Reich. Finally, in the Far East Soviet naval forces would have a role to play in the defeat of Japanese forces – and a key role in the acquisition of not only the southern part of Sakhalin but also the Kurile Islands that remain Russian to this day. The naval war in the Far East will be considered very briefly in Chapter 23, but this chapter will look at the role played by the Soviet navy in the war against Nazi Germany and her allies in the West.

(*Above*) Sputnik 952. Throughout the war Soviet light naval forces saw considerable action. In the interwar period these forces were developed before Stalin had ambitions to create an 'Ocean-Going' fleet during the 1930s – and before the subsequent need to divert productive resources to the Red Army curtailed such ambitions. In this photograph a G-5 torpedo boat is shown some-where off Odessa in August 1941. Although Germany had few naval assets in the Black Sea – getting them there was a major problem – her ally Romania did have limited naval forces in the region. These G-5 boats were not a particularly good design, because torpedoes had to be released off the back of the vessel in what was a slightly bizarre quirk. Their streamlined form did, however, give them a high top speed in suitable water, and also made them rather photogenic! This particular vessel seems to have survived the war.

(*Opposite, above*) Sputnik 59526. Although Stalin had ambitious plans for the production of new Soviet battleships in the 1930s, none of those laid down was ever completed. This left the Soviet navy with three pre-revolutionary battleships inherited from the former Tsarist fleet. Limited modernisation of these vessels could not hide the fact that they were very much outdated by the Second World War, having a top speed of only 21.5 knots in the case of *Parizhskaia kommuna*. Nonetheless, these battleships were equipped with twelve 12-inch guns, making them useful platforms for the fire-support of ground forces if they could be protected from enemy air and naval threats. Here the battleship *Parizhskaia kommuna* (renamed *Sevastopol'* in 1943) fires her guns – in all likelihood in support of ground forces – on 15 September 1941 somewhere off the city after which she was initially named and would be named again from 1943.

(*Opposite, below*) Sputnik 932. Here is the battleship *Parizhskaia kommuna* again, this time during the summer of 1942. The photograph seems to have been taken from a heavy cruiser, probably *Molotov*. If the date given for the photograph of August 1942 is correct, then she is pictured at anchor at Poti in Georgia, with Sevastopol' having fallen by this time. Interestingly, this vessel was modified to carry tanks, as the Soviet high command considered using her to ferry twenty-five KV-1 heavy tanks to the besieged city of Sevastopol' at the end of May 1942. Probably because of the risk that she might be sunk by German air attack, this plan was not carried out.[12]

(*Above*) Sputnik 58773. The defence of Sevastopol' was a protracted affair lasting from the end of October 1941 through to the beginning of July 1942, when it was finally captured by German forces. Soviet naval forces played a role in the city's defence not only in providing fire-support for ground forces, but also in bringing in supplies and personnel – and evacuating the wounded, personnel and materiel, particularly when its fall was imminent. Here the aged Tsarist-era light cruiser *Krasnii Kavkaz* is shown loading Red Army personnel and equipment including an anti-tank gun in December 1941; according to the caption provided with the photograph she was bound for Sevastopol'. In December she indeed ferried men and materiel into Sevastopol' on a number of occasions, including troops and equipment of the 79th Special Rifle Brigade, but also ran missions to Novorossiisk.[13]

(*Opposite*) Sputnik 611112. The Soviet destroyer force was particularly heavily involved in supporting besieged Soviet forces in port cities in the Black Sea, where their speed gave them an advantage over larger vessels as supply runners and in hit-and-run attacks, and where they had greater firepower and lifting capacity than their lighter brethren. Here the Type 7U destroyer *Soobrazitel'nii* is shown somewhere off Sevastopol' on 23 April 1942. In the foreground are some of her anti-aircraft guns – two 37mm automatic and one outdated 45mm semi-automatic – soon to be replaced by an additional 37mm gun. In practice such warships never had enough anti-aircraft firepower, and were particularly vulnerable to air attack if caught in daylight. In one particularly unfortunate incident for Soviet naval forces in October 1943 the Flotilla Leader *Khar'kov* with the destroyers *Besposhchadnii* and *Sposobnii* were attacked by German dive-bombers as they were returning from shelling the ports of Feodosiia and Yalta in the Crimea at night. Caught in daylight without fighter cover on their way back to Tuapse in the Caucasus (just down the coast from Novorossiisk), all three warships were sunk with the loss of 780 lives. [GPW, p. 137]

(*Opposite, above*) Sputnik 1214. Here the flotilla leader *Tashkent* – which amounted to a very large destroyer or very light cruiser – is loading munitions in all likelihood bound for Sevastopol' sometime in the early summer of 1942 in the Black Sea. On 2 July 1942 she was sunk in a German air attack on Novorossiisk, having been badly damaged at sea on her return from Sevastopol' a few days earlier when she had to be towed back to port. On 24 June alone she had delivered 1,142 personnel and equipment of the 142nd Rifle Brigade along with 10 tons of concentrated foodstuffs to Sevastopol', and picked up 2,100 wounded to be taken back to Novorossiisk.[14]

(*Opposite, below*) Sputnik 127. Soviet naval vessels were particularly vulnerable to air attack if they were caught in their bases unable to take evasive action to try to avoid enemy bombs. This picture taken on 10 June 1942 shows the Type 7U destroyer *Svobodnii*, sunk at her mooring in Sevastopol'. Having been hit by nine bombs, her fate was sealed by an ammunition explosion. *Svobodnii* or *Tashkent* were not the highest profile victims of German air strikes against ports – the battleship *Marat*, for example, was effectively sunk by German aircraft off Kronstadt near Leningrad on 23 September when hits by two 1,000kg bombs led to an ammunition explosion. The remaining section of *Marat* would, however, continue to function as an artillery battery![15]

(*Above*) Sputnik 5990888. Safer at sea – and particularly in the mist – are a 'Kirov' Class cruiser – probably *Molotov* - and a Type 7U destroyer – shown here in the Black Sea off the Crimea on 15 July 1942. Such conditions did, however, bring their own problems, such as navigational issues. Note the substantial number of anti-aircraft guns on the cruiser – an anti-aircraft armament heavily augmented for this class as a result of wartime experience.

Sputnik 62639. Here naval 'reconnaissance' troops are boarding a dinghy on 24 September 1942 from a submarine, somewhere off the Ukraine. Soviet naval forces were used extensively for disembarking raiders and 'reconnaissance' forces along enemy-occupied coastline. Soviet reconnaissance forces all too often ended up as raiders – such was the culture regarding the activities of so-called 'reconnaissance' troops. The light machine gun carried by the sailor at the front of the dinghy is testimony to the very broad interpretation of 'reconnaissance' amongst Soviet forces.

Sputnik 59767. This picture, showing crew members racing to their torpedo boats on 2 September 1943 somewhere near Novorossiisk, highlights how as a result of German activity many Soviet naval resources were not based at the sort of permanent facilities at which they had been based before the German invasion. At this point Novorossiisk was still in German hands, despite the fact that the Red Army had advanced well to the west through the Ukraine. Novorossiisk had been captured by German forces back in September 1942 as they advanced into the Caucasus, and was finally liberated later in September 1943. Even when ports such as Novorossiisk were recaptured, it would be some time before they could be used as bases again after both the retreating Red Army and then retreating Axis forces had destroyed facilities in them.

(*Above*) Sputnik 667. The Soviet Northern Fleet saw considerable activity during the Great Patriotic War, with the region gaining increased importance over pre-war Soviet expectations because it was the principal conduit for the delivery of Allied Lend-Lease aid during the early part of the war. Soviet submarines had sustained access to German targets off Norway, with it being claimed that the Soviet submarine *K-21* had attacked the battleship *Tirpitz* in July 1942 with a spread of four torpedoes, although German forces were unaware that they had been attacked. Here a 'K' Class submarine is shown at its mooring in the principal naval base for the Northern Fleet at Poliarnoe near Murmansk. In the background to the right is a Type 7 destroyer.

(*Opposite*) Sputnik 230. Here a Type 7 destroyer is pictured at sea amongst the ice that typified the seas of the Soviet north beyond the reaches of the Gulf Stream. The visible crew members are clearly dressed for the cold. For much of the year the White Sea was completely frozen over, meaning that the port of Arkhangel'sk was not used as a destination for convoys for part of the year even where icebreakers were available. The waters off the port of Murmansk to the north-west, although further north, were warmed by the Gulf Stream. Icebreakers were certainly a necessity for transit along the Northern Sea route across the north of Russia even during the summer months.

(*Above*) Sputnik 1565. In somewhat more pleasant weather a Soviet 'S' Class submarine, *S-17*, is shown probably returning to its base at Poliarnoe. Construction of the submarine had begun deep inside Russia at Gorkii in 1939 (now Nizhnii Novgorod), but after she had been floated through inland waterways she was completed at Factory 402 at Molotovsk, now Severodvinsk, near Murmansk. The date provided for this photograph is June 1942, although *S-17* wasn't in service at that time, suggesting the photograph was taken much later, possibly at the end of the war. In the foreground is a pair of Large Submarine Hunter vessels, provided by the US under the Lend-Lease agreement. What appears to be *BO-215* on the left didn't enter service with the Northern Fleet until August 1944. The Northern Fleet was a recipient of significant Lend-Lease aid as well as receiving the US cruiser *Milwaukee* and the British battleship *Royal Sovereign* – in Soviet service *Murmansk* and *Arkhangel'sk* respectively – in lieu of Italian reparations after Italy left the war.

(*Opposite, above*) Sputnik 4718. Soviet riverine forces were active not only on major Soviet rivers but also the major navigable rivers of Eastern Europe. Here a pair of armoured cutters are pictured on the Danube near Belgrade by a destroyed bridge. The date for this picture is 19 October 1944. Note how the main armaments on the cutters are in fact in tank turrets as fitted to earlier versions of the legendary T-34 tank. Such cutters could provide useful fire-support during operations such as major river crossings, as well as ferrying troops. In order to get to the Danube these cutters often faced long journeys, with many of them manufactured well to the east at Astrakhan and shipped westwards by rail.

(*Opposite, below*) Sputnik 1561. Here Soviet infantrymen are shown disembarking from a similar cutter to that shown in Sputnik 4718 somewhere near Budapest in February 1945. Budapest is also on the Danube, on which the Soviet Navy had the Danube Flotilla of light naval vessels such as this. This particular cutter (*BK-433*) entered service with the flotilla in April 1944, and ultimately ended up as an exhibit outside the Central Museum of the Armed Forces in Moscow in 1979, where it can still be seen today. Naval light craft were even used on the river Spree in Berlin in April 1945 as shown in Sputnik 159 in Chapter 22.

Chapter 8

Counter-attack: the Soviet Winter Offensive of 1941–1942

This chapter brings us back to dry land and to late 1941, when despite numerous stunning defeats over huge concentrations of Soviet troops, German chances of a knockout blow against the Soviet Union were diminishing rapidly. Although in late November 1941 the German Wehrmacht was nominally at least still on the offensive near Moscow, analysis of actions on the ground clearly shows that German offensive operations had all but run out of steam by this point. Although a freezing of the mud that had slowed down movement in the autumn had brought a brief period of greater mobility to all vehicles in November, deep snow by the later part of December would soon once again make going difficult for most forms of transport. Local Red Army counter-attacks against weary German forces were increasingly frequent in late November and early December, even before the opening of a full counter-offensive near Moscow during the weekend of 5–7 December 1941 – one of the most pivotal weekends of the war. That weekend Japan would attack the United States at Pearl Harbor, soon followed by Hitler's misguided declaration of war on the United States. Soviet offensive operations near Moscow from that weekend onwards quickly gained back territory from German forces as Hitler ordered his troops to dig in and hold ground. Under the circumstances, this decision may have saved much of the German army near Moscow, because with German troops often tenaciously defending key settlements that tended to be on transport arteries, it proved difficult for Soviet forces that had broken through on their flanks to resupply or move artillery up to support breakthroughs in the German lines. Initial Soviet successes had, however, given Stalin a sense of optimism about Soviet chances of a decisive blow against German forces that winter that would prove counter-productive. Despite mounting losses, Stalin – apparently against his general's advice – ordered the Red Army to push forward in offensive operations not only around Moscow but across the whole of Germany's Eastern Front. Through-out the remainder of the winter and into the period of the spring thaw Soviet forces hammered away at German positions with only limited success, but at horrendous cost in men and materiel.

During the battles around Moscow as a whole (that is, from the beginning of October to late April 1942) one Russian author has recently put the cost for the

Red Army at a staggering 1.6–1.66 million 'irrecoverable losses' – that is, those killed, missing, captured or died of wounds during casualty evacuation. Not that the Wehrmacht got off lightly, suffering in the region of 1.09–1.19 million similar losses, but for the Red Army these losses were on top of the millions already lost in the previous summer across the whole front. Retrospectively we can suggest that as a proportion of forces committed to the fighting German losses were more severe – as high as 52 per cent compared to as high as 35 per cent for the Red Army – but this very cold comfort was not available to the Soviet population at the time.[16] Nonetheless, despite having a higher population, the Soviet Union could not afford to squander human resources at the rate it was doing so – having lost more than 3 million troops alone captured by German forces by the end of 1941.[17] Just as German forces had failed to defeat the Soviet Union in Operation 'Barbarossa' during the summer of 1941 as hoped, and indeed had failed to do so when the initial timetable was extended with Operation 'Typhoon', so the Red Army had failed to crush the Wehrmacht during the winter of 1941/1942 as Stalin had optimistically sought. The war could not be won quickly by either side, and would drag on for another three years.

Sputnik 391. The first picture of this chapter shows Soviet artillery in action at the very beginning of December 1941 near Kalinin (now Tver'), to the north-west of Moscow. Although it is not clear whether they are supporting troops on the offensive or defensive, it serves as a reminder that the offensive operations of 5 December onwards did not suddenly take place out of the blue, but on the ground will have seemed more of a part of what went before than might be seen to be the case with the value of hindsight. Local attacks and counter-attacks characterised the first few days of December near Moscow. This picture is of interest to the equipment buff because it shows troops using mountain guns – ageing 76.2mm Model 1909 mountain guns that were used during the First World War and the Russian Civil War. Soviet forces made good use of even older equipment in late 1941. Most examples of this gun type were lost during the war.

(*Above*) Sputnik 2565. Soviet troops pass through a liberated town during the early phases of the Moscow counter-offensive on 6 December 1941. The troops in the picture seem to be well provided for with winter equipment, although the Red Army was experiencing shortages of such equipment at this time due to a combination of demand and stocks lost to enemy action. Note the horse-drawn sled in the background, behind which is what appears to be a horse-drawn field kitchen.

(*Overleaf*) Sputnik 435. Back in Chapter 5 Sputnik 2549 (see p. 65) shows Soviet cavalry on the attack in deep snow prior to the weekend of 5–7 December 1941. Cavalry units would have a major role to play in Soviet offensive operations that were part of the wider counter-offensive near Moscow from that crucial weekend onwards. In this photograph cavalry identified as being part of General Belov's cavalry corps (see Sputnik 2517 back in Chapter 4 (see p. 50)) are shown on the attack on 5 December 1941. Whether posed or not – there is no evidence in this picture of enemy counter-action – this photo gives some idea of what a Soviet cavalry attack on a German-defended settlement in early December might have looked like, at least with the cavalry at some distance away from and not being cut down by the concentrated small arms fire that would have been characteristic of an organised defence. The mobility of such cavalry at least gave scope for such troops to work around enemy defences if they were not all-round, but increasingly they were as German forces defended 'islands' located in a 'sea' of Soviet-dominated snow and forest. A cavalry charge such as this would only have some chance of success if appropriately supported by other arms, including tanks and artillery. Support from the latter in particular would often not be as forthcoming, however, if cavalry pushed on deep into German lines across the fields of deep snow, through which it would have been difficult for the artillery to follow and be resupplied. On 5 December Belov's corps was engaged in fighting to the north-east of Tula, and would on 8 December receive the honour of a Guards designation. As of 4 December the corps – with two cavalry divisions and corps headquarters – was significantly understrength, with the two cavalry divisions having a combined strength of 11,650 instead of the 'list' strength of 16,198.[18] Losses from mid-November through to 7 December had been heavy: 1,639 killed, 3,863 wounded and 176 missing.[19]

(**Opposite, above**) Sputnik 2548. Once again this picture shows Soviet cavalry during the Moscow counter-offensive, this time slightly later, on 15 December 1941. This is one of my favourite pictures from the war, in part because it has such a Russian 'feel' with the Orthodox church and landscape, but also because it has such an early war feel with the cavalrymen still wearing *Budenovka* hats against the cold even if they have their helmets strapped to their saddles. You can almost hear the crows cawing from the trees! The cavalrymen here are once again from Belov's cavalry corps. By the second half of January 1942 Belov's force consisted of in the region of 28,000 men – five cavalry (three light) and two rifle divisions, along with five ski battalions. With only eight tanks – and limited artillery assets – the corps was manoeuvrable but lacking punch – and particularly if the infantry and artillery were trailing behind. Belov's force was tasked with taking the key town of Viaz'ma, but was unable to do so. [RASWW, pp. 313–15]

(**Opposite, below**) Sputnik 1161. As Soviet offensive operations were making progress near Moscow, they were also doing so closer to Leningrad and in the south on the approaches to the Caucasus. At this time a major landing in the Crimea was supposed also to relieve the city of Sevastopol', then under siege. Here Soviet naval infantry are shown fighting for the town of Feodosia on the south-eastern side of the Crimea after the landings. The Kerch'-Feodosia Landing Operation would quickly become a major débâcle for the Red Army, with the landings contained by Axis forces and the Soviet pocket on the eastern part of the Crimea destroyed in May 1942.

(*Above*) Sputnik 2516. During the winter Soviet ski troops became a major thorn in the side for German forces with their ability to rapidly penetrate between German strongpoints and encircle them. However, as with their cavalry counterparts, their lack of organic fire-support would hamper their ability to tackle well-entrenched opposition. Here ski troops are shown near Tikhvin east of Leningrad on 11 December 1941. The fighting near Tikhvin saw German attempts to link up with the Finns and widen the encirclement of Leningrad defeated. It is worthy of note that the ski troops here do not have the white camouflage smocks that are almost iconic of the winter offensives from 1941 onwards. Such troops would, one would hope, have been some of the first in line for such smocks, highlighting that they were not as widely available as Soviet newsreel footage of the time might sometimes appear to suggest.

(*Opposite, above*) Sputnik 572. In this photograph ski troops embark on a reconnaissance mission somewhere near Leningrad in February 1942. Such troops were ideally suited to reconnaissance – which for the Red Army in practice often meant raiding behind enemy lines. This unit is well-equipped with PPSh sub-machine guns that were starting to become available in large numbers, giving Soviet forces much more firepower at close quarters. They are also wearing suitable clothing for their mission.

(*Opposite, below*) Sputnik 621. In order to increase mobility in deep snow, Soviet forces would employ the novel *aerosan* or air sled during the winter of 1941/1942. Here an air sled 'Destruction Unit' is shown on the North-Western Front during February 1942 at a time when Soviet forces were on the offensive across most of Germany's Eastern Front. The limitations of such a unit are perhaps apparent in the picture. Although very mobile, the sleds are armed only with machine guns and lack armour – making them useful for at best hit-and-run attacks. Air sleds were also apparently used for resupply, although their payloads were clearly limited. By 1 January 1942 twelve air sled battalions had reportedly been sent to the front lines, each one consisting of 40–50 sleds and 90–100 personnel. [RASWW, p. 323] That their use was not notable during subsequent winters of the war suggests that they were not necessarily deemed worth the investment.

(*Above*) Sputnik 785. The cow lends this picture something of a domestic feel, and you might be excused for thinking that those pictured here are partisans. In fact a colonel of the 4th Airborne Corps is receiving reconnaissance information as his brigade commissar looks on, early in 1942. The Moscow counter-offensive was one instance where the Red Army used parachute forces as intended – that is, by dropping them ahead of forces on the offensive. At the beginning of the war the Red Army had three airborne corps in the Soviet Union's western military districts, although there would never be enough transport aircraft to use them on a large scale. Like the cavalry, the airborne forces lacked heavy equipment and there were problems in resupplying them behind enemy lines. The airborne forces dropped near Moscow in early 1942 were supposed to facilitate the advance of the 33rd and 43rd Armies and indeed of General Belov's cavalry corps. Eventually Belov's corps did link up with the 8th Airborne Brigade [RASWW, pp. 317–18], which increased the cavalry's numerical strength but did not bring the sort of firepower that would enable them to deal with either German armoured or well entrenched forces, since Belov's force of late January had left behind its infantry divisions, heavy equipment and baggage train as it tried to take advantage of the cavalry's mobility. Although lacking potency, Soviet airborne forces continued to operate in the German rear for some time, and were also committed near Demiansk below Leningrad. In neither instance did they have the impact hoped of them.

(*Opposite, above*) Sputnik 669433. Both sides in the Great Patriotic War were heavily reliant on the horse throughout the war, the Red Army particularly so during 1941–1942. Here a 76.2mm Model 1939 Divisional gun (USB) is being pulled by a horse team somewhere near Moscow in late December 1941. The beauty of the trees encased in snow and ice provides something of a contrast with the weapon of war passing by. Fortunately the snow here does not appear to be sufficiently deep to seriously hamper movement, and the gun and limber also have the advantage of having pneumatic tyres. In deep snow with wooden wheels progress would have been much more difficult. Much as was the case for the F-22 gun, stocks of the USB would be largely expended by the end of the war, as the USB was not produced from 1943 onwards. Once again, seeing such a weapon in a picture is one clue as to when the picture was probably taken.

(*Below*) Sputnik 1166. Artillery losses for the Red Army during 1941 were sufficiently high not only for the Red Army to draw on antiquated weapons but for there to be a continued need to take advantage of captured German weapons throughout the winter of 1941/1942. Here Soviet artillerymen fire a German 105mm gun against its previous owners somewhere in the Kaluga region during the winter of 1941/1942.

(*Above*) Sputnik 436. As the first picture in this chapter including a Soviet tank we have a KV-1 tank crossing over an iced-up river somewhere near Kalinin to the north-west of Moscow in February 1942. Not only was the KV-1 tank difficult for German forces to destroy with most of the anti-tank guns available at the time, but it also had good cross-country capabilities – including in deep snow – thanks to its wide tracks. Nonetheless, at more than 40 tons it would often not be possible to be confident that even the thickest ice would hold its weight. The large building in the background certainly shows signs of heavy fighting.

(*Opposite, above*) Sputnik 560. Somewhat later in this picture – probably at the tail end of the Moscow counter-offensive – we see a T-34 tank of the Kalinin Front in action in forest terrain. T-34 production had been significantly disrupted by the Axis invasion at a time when production was being ramped up, and it would be into the spring of 1942 before productive capacity would recover and be sufficient to make the T-34 truly ubiquitous. Total production of the T-34 tank had been just over 3,000 in 1941. During 1942 – despite the destruction of the key Stalingrad Tractor Factory – production would be 12,527 for 1942 as a whole. [GPW, p. 186] The destroyed vehicle on the right is a German StuG assault gun. Its short-barrelled gun intended for infantry support would be replaced in later models in order to give it a much better anti-tank capability to allow it to deal with the T-34 and KV-series tanks.

(*Opposite, below*) Sputnik 589. The final two photographs in this chapter show fighting in the same area at a similar time. This first picture shows troops of the Soviet Western Front fighting near the town of Iukhnov to the south-east of Viaz'ma in a picture dated 5 March 1942. On that day the town was liberated by Soviet forces, although heavy fighting in the area would continue into the following month as Soviet forces sought to press on to Viaz'ma to no avail and at terrible cost.

Sputnik 281. This second photograph seems to have been taken at a similar time as Sputnik 589, and shows Soviet troops in a heavily damaged part of Iukhnov. Note the fact that the soldier on the right of the picture is using a German MP 40 sub-machine gun. With the increasing availability of the Soviet PPSh this would be less likely as the war progressed, as in some ways the German weapon was inferior. In fact, in 1942 it would be increasingly likely that German troops would be seen using the PPSh with its larger magazine.

Chapter 9

In the Enemy Rear: the Soviet Partisan Movement

During the winter of 1941/1942 Soviet efforts to reach Viaz'ma and destroy the German forces maintaining a foothold close to Moscow involved protracted heavy fighting that only petered out with the spring thaw. Not only were cavalry and airborne units operating behind German lines as part of this effort, but also partisans. Russia already had a long history of partisan warfare by 1941, including peasant resistance to Napoleon's invasion of 1812 as well as of irregular warfare during the Russian Civil War. Just who exactly constituted a partisan can be unclear. Although partisans are often seen as being those who are not uniformed members of the armed forces who are fighting an enemy, in both 1812 and the Great Patriotic War partisan forces were often led and stiffened by regular forces. It certainly suited the Soviet government to present what became the Soviet partisan movement as a 'popular' movement that had sprung up as an expression of popular resistance to the German invasion, although most of the early partisans were Party and state officials or Red Army personnel. After confused early stages of the partisan war that saw the Red Army, Communist Party and NKVD all sponsor 'partisan' units in enemy-occupied territory, in 1942 the Partisan Movement was formally developed as a Party-led organisation that would increasingly serve the needs of the Red Army for disruption in the enemy rear and reconnaissance information. Alongside these partisans there were also Red Army units operating behind enemy lines – reconnaissance troops and what would now be described as special forces. By 1942 partisans would temporarily at least be able to control huge swathes of German-occupied territory before at a certain point German forces led anti-partisan operations against them. It was very difficult for German forces to eradicate the partisan threat in a particular region, where more often than not they could only disrupt partisan forces that would often re-emerge in the same areas sometime later. It would, however, be 1943 before partisan numbers really took off in the face of German forced-labour conscription, brutal anti-partisan policies and in areas with a Jewish population anti-Jewish activity under the auspices of the Final Solution. By this point of the war going over to the partisans was made easier by the fact that it was increasingly apparent that Germany was losing the war.

As of 15 February 1944 the Soviet Partisan Movement as a whole – excluding the Ukraine – had officially lost 30,047 killed and missing out of 208,206 officially accounted-for participants. The actual number of deaths and of *de facto* participants will have been significantly higher. [RASWW, p. 286] Alongside partisan deaths many tens of thousands of Soviet civilians were killed by Axis forces in occupied territory, often as retribution for partisan activity in a particular area. At the same time German forces – led by the *Einsatzgruppen* – sought to implement the Final Solution to the Jewish question, which by 1942 increasingly meant the mass extermination of the Jewish populations of Europe. This chapter primarily looks at the Soviet war behind German lines; the concentration camps and the Final Solution will rear their ugly heads in pictures later when Soviet troops liberated some of them towards the end of the war.

(*Below*) Sputnik 965. The first picture of this chapter shows a Red Army commander showing new recruits to a partisan unit one of the weapons that they might be fighting with somewhere in the Smolensk region at the end of August 1941. Although many of the men shown here will have had some sort of military training – either having served for a period in the Red Army or had some sort of pre-conscription military training – for some of them it could have been some time ago. He is probably showing them his own pistol – they will more likely be using rifles such as that being held by one of the recruits on the left. Lightly armed and clothed, many such units would head off into the forests that summer. Few of these units would still be in operation by the end of the year, as German activity or the hostile winter conditions they faced by then saw them either destroyed or seeking to make their way back to Soviet lines.

(*Opposite, above*) Sputnik 1534. Soviet partisans head off on an assignment somewhere in German-occupied Soviet territory during the late summer of 1941. Note how they are largely armed with rifles, although there is a light machine gun in the first cart. Such a unit may have been able to disrupt German activity in remote areas, but would have had little hope when facing a German unit with any sort of firepower.

(*Below*) Sputnik 217. Here young Soviet partisans in the Pskov region are shown in position with a captured light machine gun. Such young people ended up joining the partisans in large numbers, in part because they were left in German-occupied territory if they were too young to have been drafted into the Red Army. Such young people were often targeted by Germany for forced labour from 1942 onwards, and the alternative was to join the partisans. Soviet partisans were compelled by circumstances to make widespread use of captured weapons throughout the war to make up for shortages in available Soviet weapons that had either been carried, flown or dropped into occupied territory. Weapons caches had been prepared in the 1930s for partisan use in the event of foreign invasion, but those responsible for such preparations seem to have been killed off during the paranoia of the Great Purges, leaving such preparations undermined.

(*Opposite*) Sputnik 5816873. The survival of partisan units depended not only on them surviving German attempts to destroy them, but also simply surviving in terms of having the necessary food and shelter when required. Much of the food eaten by partisans came from the local population of the areas in which they were operating – sometimes willingly provided, sometimes not. In this picture partisans are being provided with food – at great risk to the woman pictured here – by a member of the local population in Belorussia in March 1942. Partisan encampments had to be in difficult-to-access areas in order to evade German counter-measures – the partisans in this instance are clearly in such an area.

(*Above*) Sputnik 61528. Particularly during the winter months it was important for the partisans to have shelter. Here a female partisan prepares food outside a makeshift shelter in a partisan encampment near Rovno in the Ukraine in the winter of 1943. Although such encampments provided shelter – and even allowed the partisans to protect some members of the local population in what sometimes became little villages – they were a liability when they tied partisans to a particular location that might be discovered and attacked by German forces. In such circumstances partisans often took heavy losses, and many non-combatant partisans were killed either during the fighting or afterwards.

(*Overleaf*) Sputnik 215. The local civilian population wasn't just important to the partisans as a source of food and new recruits, but also as a source of information. Here a member of the local civilian population is apparently showing a group of partisans the route to get to German forces nearby during the winter of 1942/1943, somewhere in the German-occupied territory of Russia. Once again, she will have been putting herself at great risk by associating with the partisans – German forces were often swift to take out their frustrations at local partisan activity on the

civilian population, and particularly if there was evidence of it providing assistance to them. If someone was hostile to Soviet power, choosing to throw their lot in with the Germans would also have been a dangerous strategy – particularly earlier in the occupation partisans killed many who collaborated with the Germans. Many of those who collaborated with German forces in rural areas were former 'Kulaks' who had lost most from the collectivisation of agriculture from the late 1920s. Some of these 'Kulaks' were provided with land in exchange for their collaboration. Note how the partisans here are all armed with sub-machine guns, by now widely available and a popular weapon with partisans.

(*Opposite, above*) Sputnik 608601. The costs of occupation were often high. The official caption for this photograph suggests that the civilians here are looking for the bodies of loved ones amongst those killed by the Germans, with a view to reburying them. This shot was taken in the recently liberated Dneprovskii District in the Ukraine in September 1943.

(*Opposite, below*) Sputnik 864064. One of the most important functions of the partisan movement was to disrupt German lines of communication to assist the Red Army at the front line. Here partisans in the Crimea prepare to destroy a section of railway line in March 1942. Although key railway lines were relatively well guarded by German forces and local collaborators, it was difficult to guarantee the security of all sections of the lines at all times. In the summer of 1943 partisans across the Soviet Union launched a major operation to destroy railways and disrupt the German rail network – an operation known as the 'War of the Rails'. Although German forces became adept at quickly replacing damaged sections of track, the 'War of the Rails' was a considerable drain on German personnel and resources, and also caused disruption to the resupply and reinforcement of the front line.

(*Opposite*) Sputnik 2451. Although the majority of partisans were young people who had been of pre-conscription age when the war began – with some partisans of conscription age having been brought into the German rear from Soviet lines – there were some who were older than either of these two groups. Here an older partisan is shown somewhere in Belorussia in April 1943. Just how useful he would have been in a dynamic combat situation with German forces is debatable, but such shots helped spread the notion that the partisan movement was one of 'all of the people' in occupied territory. The young people in the background are more typical in age for a partisan unit. This unit seems to be fairly well provided for in terms of clothing and equipment, to the extent that it even has a 76.2mm Model 1927 Regimental Gun (shown behind the older partisan). Whilst such a weapon would undoubtedly have been useful in action against German forces, moving it through the sort of terrain that partisans often moved through would have been challenging to say the least, as would keeping it supplied with ammunition. Some partisan units built makeshift airstrips in the forest for resupply, but such assets tied partisans to particular areas and made their discovery by German forces all the more likely.

(*Above*) Sputnik 61709. Mounted troops were used by both partisans and German forces in the partisan war. Here, in a scene reminiscent of a Wild West movie, young Ukrainian partisans on horseback prepare to move off on some sort of mission in June 1943. Mounted troops were particularly suited to the scouting role, where they could of course cover a lot of ground quickly and relatively quietly.

(*Opposite*) Sputnik 1165. Mounted troops also allowed some partisan units to launch deep pene-trations into enemy-held territory, the most famous instance of which is probably the raid led by Sidor Kovpak in the Ukraine to the west of the Dnepr as far as the Carpathian Mountains during the second half of 1943. Kovpak was a locally well-known veteran of the Civil War in the Sumi region of the Ukraine, who would once again engage in irregular warfare during the Great Patriotic War. Here he is shown – bearded and wearing the black hat in the centre of the picture – with a column of his forces sometime in 1943, and probably during a raid somewhere in the Sumi, Orlov, Briansk and Kursk regions in the winter of 1942/1943. It is testimony to the sheer size of the territories concerned that Kovpak's forces as pictured here were not located and destroyed by German forces, especially since the long column including sleds pictured here was far from manoeuvrable compared to mounted troops on their own.

(*Above*) Sputnik 494. Here is a slightly later picture of some of Kovpak's partisans, taken in the Kiev region in March 1943. Of note is not only the youthfulness of the partisans pictured here, but that they are well-equipped with automatic weapons, from the PPSh sub-machine gun to the DP light machine gun first introduced in 1927 being carried by a number of the partisans in the foreground. I am not convinced of the wisdom of wearing a German field blouse, as in the case of the third partisan from the left in the front row!

(*Above*) Sputnik 851357. Some partisan units were sent from Soviet lines into the German rear, with many of their members either being military personnel or serving as partisans as an alternative to serving in the Red Army. Such units as the one shown here in February 1943 in German-occupied territory in front of the North-Western Front were usually very well equipped and militarily far more capable than those locally raised in German-occupied territory. Even in the case of the latter, qualified and specialised personnel were sent from Soviet lines to assist them, and as the war progressed such units were 'professionalised' and 'militarised', more and more taking on the form of military units operating in the German rear complete with a larger number of uniformed personnel. In this picture note that the personnel are clearly of conscription age, are wearing Red Army clothing, and are generally well provided for, including with the radio set in the foreground. A lack of radio sets early in the war meant that partisan units were often unable to provide timely intelligence to those on the Soviet side of the front line. By 1943 most partisan units of any size were provided with at least one radio set. The downside of having radio communications was that it gave German forces the possibility of intercepting communications and triangulating the location of a partisan unit from its radio transmissions.

(*Opposite*) Sputnik 2278743. Alongside partisans there were other Soviet troops operating on German and Axis-occupied territory. Some of those troops were Red Army scouts, such as Senior Sergeant Frolchenko pictured here in August 1943 after he had participated in the Battle of Kursk. Frolchenko fought from the Battle of Stalingrad through to the Battle of Berlin. He is wearing a camouflage coverall as frequently worn by Red Army scouts during the latter half of the war, has a pair of binoculars, and is armed with the by this point ubiquitous PPSh sub-machine gun. Although such reconnaissance troops were more likely to be found closer to the front line, they sometimes penetrated deep into enemy-held territory.

Sputnik 1230. The final picture in this chapter shows Leningrad region partisans meeting up with advancing forces of the Red Army at Luga in the Leningrad region in February 1944. Although the liberation of their operating areas was no doubt a joyous moment for partisan units, the war was for many of those in such units not over on liberation. By the later part of the war the Red Army was all too often desperately short of infantrymen, and many partisans would find themselves drafted into the Red Army as their partisan units were overrun by advancing Soviet forces.

Chapter 10

Soviet Women and the War Effort

Although the Soviet government had championed women's liberation during the 1920s, by the late 1930s it had backtracked on the notion of sexual equality. Even during the 1920s it had not gone as far as to allow women to undertake combat roles in the armed forces as there was little need for them to do so – in the early 1920s the financial exigencies of the period meant that the armed forces were being cut, not looking for an additional category of recruits. Consequently, when Nazi Germany invaded the Soviet Union on 22 June 1941 there were few women in the Red Army – the only area in which significant numbers of women were employed being the medical services, and even then the preference was to keep them as far from the fighting as possible. There were, however, significant numbers of women working in industry, where women would rapidly increase as a proportion of the workforce. Also, as men were conscripted into the armed forces, women had to make up for the shortfall in agricultural labour, where human effort also had to replace some that had been provided by horses drafted into the Red Army in huge numbers. Women of all ages were also employed when the situation demanded it in building defences in a desperate attempt to halt Axis forces before Moscow and Leningrad. Very quickly the manpower situation in the Red Army started to deteriorate as well, and there were significant numbers of young women available who were both keen to serve in uniform and often had meaningful pre-conscription training through organisations such as OSOAVIAKHIM (see Chapter 1) and the youth wing of the Party, the Komsomol. Such women were initially used in what were technically non-combat roles – as drivers, telecommunications operators and as nurses and *fel'dsher* (paramedics). Although these roles did not involve killing the enemy, they frequently put young women in the line of fire. A limited number of women did find themselves more directly involved in the killing of the enemy in militia units hastily organised to face the enemy advance or as partisans, although the numbers involved were proportionally small. By 1942, however, once the scale of manpower losses in 1941 had sunk in, far greater numbers of young women were sought for roles within the Red Army and indeed became involved in the partisan movement. By now it had been accepted that women would be employed in some 'combat' roles. Regarding anti-aircraft guns, for example, the Soviet Union did not have the sort of qualms about women being employed as anti-aircraft gunners as in the West, where even in Britain – where women did crew anti-aircraft guns –

a line was drawn over women actually firing the gun and hence being directly involved in killing. In the Soviet armed forces relatively small numbers of women were employed in what were clearly front-line combat roles – from the crews of light bombers employed at night to snipers – many of the women had shown their marksmanship skills before the war in the Komsomol. There was pressure from women for their employment at the front line within the ground forces to move beyond isolated instances to the employment of whole units of female combatants. Indeed, a 6,983-strong women's rifle brigade was formed but was not allowed to see action at the front line, instead being employed in rear-area security. [RASWW, p. 327] The Soviet-sponsored Polish armed forces did, however, cross the line in employing female combat units in what were clearly combat operations at the front, since for them manpower shortages were even more acute until they reached Polish territory. Although historians have disagreed on the exact number of women who saw service with the Red Army during the Great Patriotic War, it is likely that approaching a million women saw military service of some sort during the war, with at least a third of these seeing service with the Soviet fronts – that is, those formations making up the front-line forces. [RASWW, pp. 324–5] Be it in the rear, or close to or at the front line, Soviet women played a far more visible role in the Soviet war effort than women in the West, and this chapter highlights the many dimensions of that role.

Sputnik 348. Although the Soviet Union already had a significant number of women in the industrial workforce prior to the Great Patriotic War, that number would increase dramatically during the war with women taking on roles that had previously typically been undertaken by men. Here in early 1943 women are working in a Leningrad factory that had been mothballed during the worst period of the blockade, to be reinstated after the siege had been partially lifted. By this time the manpower shortage in the Red Army – and in particularly in front-line infantry units – was starting to become even more acute, meaning that men who had previously been in protected work were sent to the front and replaced by women.

Sputnik 892437. Large numbers of women in the Soviet Union were, even more so than was the case in Britain, for example, involved in munitions production. Here a young woman is engaged in the production of mortar bombs in a Moscow factory sometime during 1942. Even before the war the Soviet working week had been increased to six days, which when combined with long hours made such factory work gruelling.

(*Above*) Sputnik 835682. Women of all ages were employed in the construction of defensive positions during the war, although in this picture the women concerned are all younger women who have been mobilised by the Communist youth organisation, the Komsomol. They are shown constructing an anti-tank ditch somewhere in the Moscow region on 8 July 1941 as it became apparent that the capital was under threat.

(*Opposite, above*) Sputnik 732. From early in the war Soviet women were employed in the air defence network, initially in local roles that included what in Britain was known as Air Raid Precautions (ARP). Here a group of young women are being employed by the Local Air Defence organisation for Leningrad. This picture was taken in May 1942 from the roof of Building Number 4 on what is now Millionnaia Street in the centre of what is now St Petersburg.

(*Opposite, below*) Sputnik 90487. It did not take long for women to start replacing men in anti-aircraft defence roles as part of the Air Defence Forces of the Soviet Union, firstly in the defences of Soviet cities and other objectives. On 25 March 1942 the Soviet State Defence Committee ordered that 100,000 young women aged 19–25 be mobilised for service in the Air Defence Forces to replace men not only in such roles as radio and telephone operators and observers, but also in crews for searchlights and anti-aircraft guns. [RASWW, p. 326] Later in the war women would be employed in such roles as part of the advancing Red Army. Here Tatiana Shmorgunova and her colleagues are shown with an optical rangefinder as part of the defences for a Soviet crossing-point over the Oder river in the heart of Germany near Berlin in late April 1945.

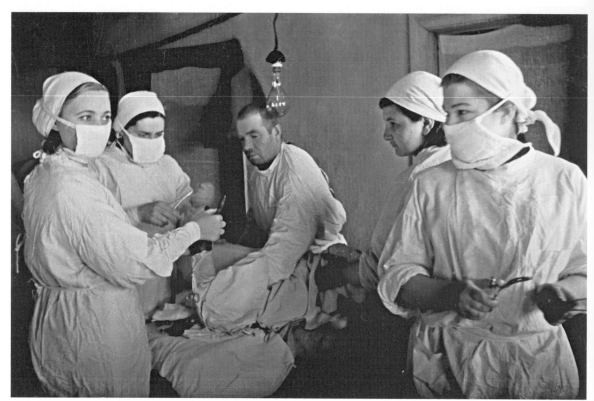

(*Above*) Sputnik 64114. Although the Red Army employed few women prior to the war, one area in which women were meaningfully represented was in military medicine, and in particular in a hospital setting. Women were not only employed as nurses and *fel'dsher* (paramedics), but as doctors: of 100,301 doctors liable for call-up in May 1941 only 36.8 per cent were men. [RASWW, p. 325] All but one of this surgical team at a medical battalion facility of the 2nd Ukrainian Front during the summer of 1943 are women. To have women serving in such units – behind the front line – was deemed appropriate even before the war. A total of 41,224 women would be conscripted into front-line military medical units during the war as a whole. [RASWW, p. 326]

(*Opposite, above left*) Sputnik 67355. Placing women in more dangerous medical roles closer to the front line was something Soviet authorities were reticent to do at the beginning of the war, but they soon changed their minds as there was a heavy demand for front-line medical personnel. Increasingly large numbers of young women volunteered for, or were conscripted into, a variety of front-line medical roles. Training to be a medic was one means by which women who were keen to join the Red Army and take a front-line role could do so during the early phases of the war. Here a female medic tends to a lightly wounded Red Army man sometime during September 1942.

(*Opposite, above right*) Sputnik 1416. Another area in which large numbers of women would be employed by the Red Army from early on in the war was in what might be described as 'house-keeping' duties, that is, undertaking such essential tasks as laundry, book-keeping and barbershop duties. Here a female barber shaves a Red Army man on the territory of the Baltic Republics during the summer of 1944.

(*Opposite, below*) Sputnik 457. One of the more dangerous non-combat roles carried out by Soviet women in the Red Army was as radio and telephone operators – a role that would frequently put them close to the fighting. Shown is a communications hub for the 138th Rifle Division during the fighting for Stalingrad in December 1942. Here men and women are operating the communications equipment from a basement of the Red October Factory. Some young women had received training for such roles in the Komsomol Communist youth organisation prior to the war.

Sputnik 42435. Perhaps one of the most famous roles for women in the Red Army – made so by footage and photographs of Maria Limanskaia at the Brandenburg Gate in Berlin at the end of the war – was as a traffic controller, that is, directing traffic at road junctions. I have chosen not to show one of the iconic images of Limanskaia since they are widely available, but of a different, unnamed, traffic controller also in Berlin at the end of the war. This image was taken on 4 May 1945.

Sputnik 68660. Soviet women were involved in combat early in the war within the Soviet partisan movement, in which typically younger women would play an increasing role as the war progressed. Here female partisans relax somewhere in Russia during September 1943. By January 1944 about 10 per cent of the officially accounted-for participants in the partisan movement seem to have been women, although it is likely that the actual proportion was significantly higher. [RASWW, p. 326]

Sputnik 2414. Perhaps the most iconic combat role for women in the Red Army was as a sniper. Many young women had become proficient markswomen in the Komsomol prior to the war, and were keen to carry their proficiency into a wartime role. Although Soviet military and political leaders were not willing to see combat units made up entirely of women engaged in the slaughter at the front line – and particularly given the potentially negative propaganda that could have resulted from pictures of the bodies of hundreds of young women killed in action – they were willing to employ women in front-line combat roles in isolated instances. Here two young female snipers of the 33rd Army of the 2nd Belorussian Front are shown in August 1944. The Central Women's School for the Preparation of Snipers created in May 1943 would send 1,061 female snipers to the front, as well as producing 407 female instructors in sniping. [RASWW, p. 327] The helmet on a stick is being used to try to lure enemy soldiers – particularly snipers – to reveal themselves.

(*Opposite*) Sputnik 825070. Before the war the Komsomol had given a select group of Soviet young people the opportunity to learn to fly. This in many ways set the scene for the activities of a limited number of female flyers during the Great Patriotic War. Perhaps the most famous female flying unit was the 588th Night Light Bomber Aviation Regiment, later becoming the 46th Guards Night Bomber Air Regiment. This unit was formed in 1941 and tasked with the harassment bombing of enemy units at night using the U-2 biplane aircraft. The unit – whose exploits were clearly used for propaganda purposes – gained something of a reputation with the enemy and earned them the nickname the 'Night Witches'. Here members of the unit are shown loading bombs on an aircraft in the summer of 1944.

(*Above*) Sputnik 63675. A limited number of Soviet women were allowed to serve as fighter pilots during the war. Hence, in the same order of the People's Commissar for Defence that had ordered the formation of the 588th Night Light Bomber Aviation Regiment on 8 October 1941, it was also ordered that a women's fighter air regiment be formed, the 586th Fighter Air Regiment.[20] Here female pilots Lidia Litviak, Katia Budanova and Masha Kuznetsova are shown with one of their Yak-1 fighter aircraft during the first half of the war – possibly by now as part of the 9th Guards Fighter Air Regiment. Even if units such as the 586th Fighter Air Regiment were in a sense tokenistic, the employment of women in such roles at all set the Soviet Union apart from the other major powers, and the combat and risks faced by such pilots was only too real. Guards Junior Lieutenant Lidia Litviak would not return from a combat mission with the 73rd Guards Fighter Air Regiment on 1 August 1943 – lost without trace alongside her male colleague Sergeant Nikolai Ugarov that same day.[21] That Lidia Litviak (along with Katia Budanova) was not kept in an all-female unit was undoubtedly testimony to her abilities as a pilot.

Sputnik 67371. The women of the Soviet-sponsored Polish Army that fought alongside the Red Army seem to have ended up being employed in unit strength in ground combat on the Eastern Front. Here female soldiers of the Women's Battalion of the 1st Polish Infantry Division 'Tadeusza Kościuszki' are shown in the division's camp near Riazan' to the south-east of Moscow in mid-July 1943. The division would receive its 'baptism by fire' at the Battle of Lenino in October 1943.

Chapter 11

'All for the Front!': the Soviet Rear

In the last chapter we had already started to look at what was going on behind the front lines of the Great Patriotic War when looking at the role of women in the Soviet war effort, and this chapter will further explore what was going in the Soviet rear to sustain the war effort. Although the Axis advance was halted and thrown back by the combat troops, they could of course not have done so without the millions of people either in uniform or otherwise toiling at various depths behind the front line. From the medical services of the armed forces to the peasantry working the fields, much of the Soviet population made some sort of contribution to victory over Germany and her allies. Food, equipment and munitions had to be produced and delivered to the front lines in a timely manner, just as the wounded had to receive medical treatment as quickly as possible and damaged equipment be repaired and thrown back into action.

Both Soviet agricultural and industrial production were severely dislocated during the early part of the war as enemy forces seized vast tracts of Soviet territory. Although the Soviet government started to evacuate factories to the East from the first days of the war, even if they were successfully loaded onto trains for their journey eastwards it would take some time to get production restarted in a new location. At least in the case of industrial concerns factories could be relocated – however, in the case of agricultural assets, animals and agricultural machinery could be evacuated but land lost to the enemy represented production lost. Production was also lost when the fighting ranged over agricultural areas, whether or not that territory was ultimately lost to the enemy for a meaningful period of time. Stalin chose suddenly to highlight the significance of loss of territory in his famous 'Not a Step Back!' order of 28 July 1942 – Order Number 227 of the People's Commissar for Defence for 1942. In the order, Stalin noted:

> Certain unintelligent people at the front comfort themselves with talk that we can retreat to the east even further, because we have a huge territory, vast quantities of land, a large population, and we will always have surplus bread …
>
> Every commander, Red Army and political worker should understand that our resources are not without limits … The territory of the Soviet Union, which has been seized and is in the process of being seized by the

enemy, is bread and other foodstuffs for the army and the rear; metals and fuel for industry; mills and factories, which are supplying the army with arms and munitions; and railway lines …

… it is time to put an end to the retreat.

Not a step back! Such should now be our principal call. [GPW, p. 101]

The loss of agricultural land was particularly severe in 1942 and into 1943 as in the summer of 1942 the Axis swept across the agricultural lands of the Ukraine and southern Russia, when a second wave of industrial dislocation also took place. By this time, however, much of the plant evacuated in 1941 was up and running again as the Soviet economic effort was thrown behind the production of armaments and munitions. As the Soviet Union gained the upper hand in the war, considerable effort had to be expended to keep the Red Army advancing, as German forces destroyed thousands of kilometres of railway lines in their wake that had to be rebuilt. The final phase of the journey of troops and supplies to the front line took place by vehicle, horse-drawn transport or, in the case of the soldiers, often by foot. Making the situation easier in one sector of concern could often make it more difficult elsewhere. The Red Army's insatiable need for horses, for example, would deprive agriculture of motive power, just as the Red Army's manpower needs would denude the working population in the country-side in particular. That the Soviet war effort held together owes something to Allied material aid – a topic for a later chapter – but also to the often heroic efforts of the Soviet population not only on the battlefield but also in the rear.

(*Opposite*) Sputnik 643. We start this chapter with photographs taken closest to the front line with wounded personnel being evacuated to the rear. Getting the wounded from the front line to hospital facilities was often very challenging in a pre-helicopter era – and particularly where there was a shortage of suitable motor vehicles. Here a dog team pulls a wounded soldier towards a hospital of the 1st Ukrainian Front, sometime in June 1944. According to Svetlana Gladish, author of *Dogs of the Fronts of the Great Patriotic War*, 4,500 dog teams were employed in casualty evacuation during the Great Patriotic War, which evacuated in the region of 600,000 wounded Red Army personnel.[22] Sadly, dogs were also used to a limited extent in a tank destruction role, although their success in this (in the process of which they were killed) seems to have been limited.

(*Above*) Sputnik 1272. Sometimes it was possible to evacuate wounded deeper into the rear by aircraft, although rank-and-file personnel would not typically have had that luxury. Certainly such aircraft were more likely to be used for figures in leadership positions. For example, on 3 December 1941 the headquarters of what would soon become the 1st Guards Cavalry Corps sent an urgent request to Nikolai Bulganin – member of the Military Soviet for the Western Front – that an ambulance aircraft be sent for the evacuation of the political commissar for the unit, Brigade Commissar Shchelakovskii, who had fallen 'seriously ill'.[23] These ambulance variants of the legendary Po-2 aircraft allowed the patient to be accompanied by a member of the medical personnel, who in the confines of the enclosed rear compartment could at least access the patient's upper body during flight. This photograph was taken in August 1943 on the Kalinin Front. Clearly casualty evacuation by aircraft required suitable terrain. On occasion it proved possible to evacuate even wounded partisans by air from makeshift landing strips – sometimes cut out of forested terrain.

(*Opposite, above*) Sputnik 662769. Here a wounded soldier has reached a field hospital of the Volkhov Front near Leningrad in December 1941. According to one set of figures provided for the Red Army's field forces, up to 1 January 1942 there were 1,532,367 wounded and shell-shocked personnel requiring treatment, along with 5,570 burns cases, 29,625 cases of frostbite and 374,298 cases of sickness, giving a staggering total of 1,941,860 cases.[24] Given such figures, it is understandable how the military-medical services struggled to deal with such numbers, in particular where there were shortages of key personnel.

(*Opposite, below*) Sputnik 662771. Here an operation is taking place in a field hospital – also of the Volkhov Front – in January 1943. There continued to be shortages in the number of surgeons available throughout the Great Patriotic War; for example, up to the end of 1942 the number of general surgeons did not reach 50 per cent of the number required according to list strengths for medical units. Nonetheless, during this first turbulent period of the war to the end of 1942, of a total of nearly 7 million casualties 4,780,815 were recorded as either returning to their units or being sent to units for those 'recovering' from wounds. By the end of 1943 there were 588 200-bed mobile surgical field hospitals alone with the Red Army's field forces.[25]

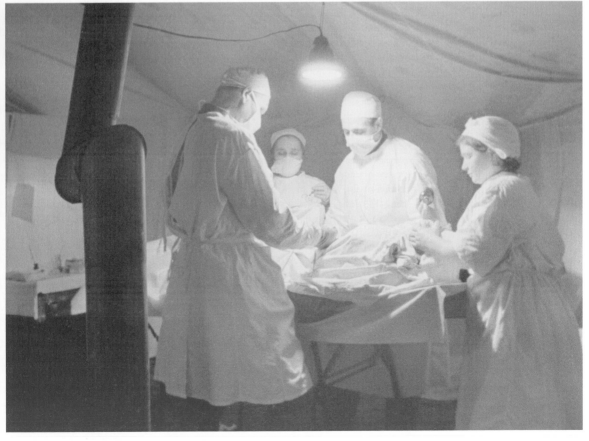

(*Above*) Sputnik 5632. Not only wounded people but damaged equipment had to be transported to the rear, and in the case of vehicles repaired. Here BA-6/10 armoured cars are undergoing repairs in a factory in Leningrad sometime during September 1941. The logistical issues surrounding returning vehicles to factories for repair should not be underestimated. As the war progressed the Red Army sought to undertake more repairs in the field, but sometimes there was no choice but to send damaged vehicles to factories in the rear.

(*Opposite, above*) Sputnik 865643. In addition to military vehicles requiring repair in the Soviet rear, another significant category for repair was railway locomotives and rolling stock. The railways were a crucial element in the Soviet war effort, be that for moving raw materials to factories, or taking finished goods and personnel to the front line. Railway locomotives were not only in need of repair through wear and tear, but also through enemy action, as trains were frequently subject to air attack. By the time this photograph was taken – in February 1945 – the German Luftwaffe's capacity to attack trains from the air had significantly diminished, but the Soviet railways had vast distances to contend with when moving and supplying the Red Army on German territory and all the way from the Arctic Circle down through to Bulgaria. The locomotive pictured here seems to be an early Soviet Eg or Esh model of the early 1920s that were produced in Germany and Sweden respectively, here being repaired at the Dzerzhinskii Factory in Voronezh. The Soviet Union produced few locomotives during the war, and although it would receive large numbers of locomotives from the United States under Lend-Lease, particularly earlier in the war those that it had on hand were not a resource to be squandered after the heavy losses of the first months of the war.

(*Opposite, below*) Sputnik 2466476. This photo – also including a railway locomotive – is of the famous Red October metallurgical factory in Stalingrad, shown as reconstructed by the time this photograph was taken in February 1944. The factory had been destroyed during fighting for the city in late 1942 and early 1943. Not only did the dislocation of industrial production by the war have a significant impact on Soviet production during late 1941 and early 1942 in particular, but the reconstruction of industry destroyed during the fighting or by the retreating Axis forces was also a drain on resources. After the defeat of Nazi Germany the Soviet Union would strip Germany of much of its surviving industrial plant as reparations for damage caused on Soviet territory.

(*Above*) Sputnik 611734. Some of the most unsung contributors to the Soviet war effort were Kolkhoz or collective farm peasants, who in far from conducive circumstances continued to produce food for the Soviet Union. With millions of men, horses and vehicles mobilised for the war, female and older collective farm peasants managed to provide the Soviet Union with some food from communal land and private plots. Much of the Soviet Union's prime agricultural land was under German occupation during the first half of the war, severely curtailing what the Soviet Union could produce, and military activity often severely disrupted the harvest in those areas over which fighting took place. Where in 1940 Soviet agriculture had produced 95.5 million tons of grains, during 1942 and 1943 production stood at only 29.7 and 29.4 million tons respectively. By the time this photograph was taken in the spring of 1944 in the Ukraine, Soviet agricultural production was on the road to a degree of recovery thanks to the liberation of agricultural lands by the Red Army, although production of grains for 1944 would still only amount to 49.1 million tons [GPW, p. 190]. Note how in this photograph ploughing is taking place with the help of cows rather than horses. Lend-Lease aid would make up for some of the shortfall in Soviet agricultural production.

(*Opposite, above*) Sputnik 5645971. That the Soviet economy was able to produce the armaments it did during the first half of the war – after the loss of sizeable territory in the more industrialised European part of the Soviet Union – constitutes something of an economic miracle. Here we see a production line for T-34 tanks at Tank Factory Number 183 in the Urals at Nizhnii Tagil in October 1942. By this point T-34 production had ramped up dramatically after industry relocated eastwards from the west of the country was back in operation. Factory Number 183 had started its life in Khar'kov, where it began producing T-34 tanks in 1940, during which the first 117 T-34 tanks were produced. After the Axis invasion, having produced more than 1,500 tanks to date in 1941, it was moved to the Urals where meaningful production restarted in 1942, by the end of which it had produced 5,684 T-34 tanks. This was just as well given that production at the Stalingrad Tractor Factory was knocked out by the fighting for the city in late 1942. During 1943 Factory Number 183 would go on to produce a further 7,466 T-34 tanks [GPW, p. 186].

(*Opposite, below*) Sputnik 634312. Here a batch of much-needed KV-1 Model 1941 tanks arrive near Moscow (Dubosekovo) in what according to the date provided with the photograph is late October 1941. During this period the Red Army was particularly short of tanks on the Moscow axis, especially heavy and medium tanks. The contribution that the tanks in this picture alone might have made to the defence of Moscow should not be underestimated. Tanks were shipped by rail from the factories, ideally not being driven for long distances before reaching the front line. The KV-1 tanks shown here are a variant with a cast turret. There was also a simplified variant of this tank with a welded turret that gave the tank a much more angular appearance.

(*Above*) Sputnik 62729. Having railway lines as close to the front line as possible was a perpetual challenge for Soviet railway troops, since as the Red Army advanced German forces destroyed what they could as they retreated. Particularly vulnerable to being destroyed were bridges, either by retreating German forces or in some instances by the Soviet air forces or partisans seeking to limit German reinforcement of, or retreat from, a particular sector of the front line. Here Soviet troops are rebuilding a bridge somewhere in Russia in March 1943. Due in part to language barriers, the non-Slavic nationalities of the Soviet Union were often disproportionately represented amongst troops carrying out such laborious rear-area functions. The speed with which such bridges and the railways could be rebuilt could play a significant role in the extent to which Soviet offensive operations could be sustained after their start dates.

(*Opposite, above*) Sputnik 978. Thousands of kilometres of railway line had to be rebuilt in the wake of the German retreat. German forces became efficient at destroying not only bridges, but also long sections of the track itself, using giant claws pulled by locomotives to tear apart the sleepers to which the track was attached. Here Soviet troops are shown rebuilding a section of track near Novorzhev in what was by 1944 the Pskov region. In addition to rebuilding sections of track, sometimes Soviet forces would add additional track to stretches of railway line in order to increase capacity.

(*Opposite, below*) Sputnik 1833. Often the Soviet advance was not along the route of railway lines, and this was certainly the case in the far north. Even where the advance could be supported by railway lines nearby, troops and supplies had to be moved from railheads to the front line, often through terrain where there were not even rudimentary roads. Here Soviet troops lay a corduroy road through the *taiga* in the Murmansk region in the far north in April 1942 that would allow wheeled vehicles to access this area even when the ground was waterlogged. As you can imagine, such roads demanded a significant amount of wood.

(*Above*) Sputnik 60230. Enemy mines were a hazard not only in battle, but for those troops following on behind the front-line troops. Millions of mines were laid by both sides during the war, and had to be cleared from key lines of communication. Here Soviet sappers clear mines on the edge of a road in late August 1943 in the aftermath of the fighting in the Kursk region. The soldier in the foreground on the left is using an electrical mine detector. As will be apparent in the final chapter of this book, the problem of mines was one that extended well into the post-war period, claiming many lives even after the war was over.

(*Opposite*) Sputnik 65896. The final photograph of this chapter puts us somewhere back near the front line where we began the chapter, and indeed at the very end of the war. Here Soviet troops are shown on a busy German road on the Berlin axis on 20 April 1945. Clearly evident is the Red Army's use of both horse-drawn and motorised transport, with both Soviet-manufactured and Allied-supplied motor vehicles in view. As will be noted later in Chapter 16, Allied-supplied motor vehicles played an important part in keeping up the Red Army's advance beyond the railheads, with what were by the end of the war ubiquitous Dodge trucks and a jeep both appearing in this shot alongside very traditional horse-drawn carts.

Chapter 12

'Not a Step Back!': Stalingrad and the Caucasus

In late 1941 the Red Army had gone from crisis on the approaches to Moscow in October to dramatic battlefield successes during the early phases of the Soviet counter-offensive near Moscow. This recovery did not, however, mean a complete transformation of Soviet fortunes. The subsequent overambitious Soviet winter counter-offensive of 1941–1942 would drag on far too long for increasingly limited gains, thanks certainly to a considerable extent to Stalin's insistence that the enemy was on the verge of being beaten and that a swift Soviet victory was possible. Although German forces had been halted before Moscow, on the approaches to the Caucasus and near Leningrad, the German armed forces and their allies not only survived the Soviet winter counter-offensives, but inflicted considerable losses on the Red Army in doing so. Certainly by the spring of 1942 conditions for ultimate German victory were far less favourable than they had been the previous year, in particular given that US industrial might was now being mobilised in earnest behind the Allied war effort. Soviet industry was also recovering from the dislocation of 1941, with at least some of the industrial plant from the west now in situ in the Urals and Central Asia. Nazi Germany was, however, far from being a spent force. Although the Soviet leadership expected that German forces would have a second attempt at capturing Moscow in the summer of 1942, Hitler's attention had shifted southwards towards the Caucasus, reflecting an acceptance of the need for resources in the inevitably more protracted war that Germany was now embroiled in. If Germany could capture the Caucasus and its oil – along with Soviet raw materials in the Donbass and the Black Earth agricultural regions of the Soviet Union on the way – then not only would what would become known as Fortress Europe be in a stronger position, but those resources would be denied to the Soviet Union.

As both sides made plans for the summer campaigning season of 1942, it was the Soviet Union that would get in the first major blow in a misguided attack in the Khar'kov region in the south in May. The failure of this attack – resulting in the destruction of a large Red Army mechanised force – set Germany and her allies up for initial success in the south as they pushed on across the Ukraine and southern Russia into the Caucasus. For Stalin, the speed of the Axis advance and the territory that their forces were acquiring were of grave concern – a concern that Stalin was for once willing to pass on to the Red Army rather than keeping up a pretence that everything was under control. Stalin's famous 'Not A Step

Back!' order of 28 July 1942 – issued in his role as People's Commissar for Defence – certainly marked a change in tone in such orders in that it was blunt in presenting the danger of the situation for the Soviet Union. Subsequently many Red Army personnel would recall how Order Number 227 was something of a 'wake-up call' for them in bringing home the urgency of the situation. [GPW, p. 100–2; RASWW, p. 354] New repressive measures to keep the Red Army fighting accompanied the order, with Stalin giving Nazi Germany praise in the order itself for its use of penal units as a disciplinary tool. That the epicentre of the fighting in the south became Stalingrad is well known, as both sides poured troops into the fighting for the city from the late summer into the autumn. Despite German forces capturing as much as 90 per cent of the city, Soviet defenders clung on to a small island of resistance in the city as on the periphery Soviet forces were massed for a counter-offensive. In the Caucasus as well the advance of German forces was halted before they had reached the principal oilfields in the far south. Hitler's gamble – to throw sizeable German forces into a headlong charge across southern European Soviet territory – had already failed as the winter set in, and even before the Soviet offensive of 19 November near Stalingrad – Operation 'Uranus' – turned failure into a débâcle.

(*Opposite, above*) Sputnik 491038. The first two photographs in this chapter capture something of the intensity and horror of combat. Here a British-supplied 'Matilda' tank – with accompanying infantry of the South-Western Front –is shown on the attack near Zmiev, south of Khar'kov, during the summer of 1942. This is certainly not a staged photograph, with a casualty certainly evident on the right-hand side of the tank, and possibly also the left. Although the Soviet practice of having infantrymen ride on tanks into battle meant that tanks were more likely to have close infantry support – and to some extent made up for shortages in armoured fighting and other vehicles to carry infantry into battle – it also resulted in heavy casualties. There is, as is clear from this photograph, little protection for infantrymen on the back of a tank, and their desperation to get off the tank into some sort of cover is very much evident.

(*Opposite, below*) Sputnik 666554. This second photograph, taken moments after 491038, shows the body of one of the infantrymen on the ground in the front-centre part of the picture, with what is quite possibly a second casualty on the far left. None of the infantrymen here has a PPSh sub-machine gun, a weapon that would become synonymous with tank-riding infantry as the war progressed. Consequently the infantrymen here would be very much dependent on the firepower of the accompanying tank when engaging enemy positions at close range.